D0371651

ADVERSITY

ADVERSITY

Elaine Cannon

Bookcraft
Salt Lake City, Utah

Copyright © 1987 by Bookcraft, Inc.

All rights reserved. This book or any part thereof may not be
reproduced in any form whatsoever, whether by graphic,
visual, electronic, filming, microfilming, tape recording, or
any other means, without the prior written permission of
Bookcraft, Inc., except in the case of brief passages
embodied in critical reviews and articles.

Library of Congress Catalog Card Number: 87-70859
ISBN 0-88494-630-4

5th Printing, 1989

Printed in the United States of America

To all those who have ever had a bad day
And to those who have faced real adversity
with shining courage
and a conquering spirit . . .
And, as well, to those who are anxious
to learn how to do just that

Contents

Preface

Do you have trouble? Are you in the midst of affliction? If so, this book is for you.

The fact that at some point in life everyone is plagued with adversity doesn't make suffering any easier to bear when you are the one hurting. Each of us wants to weather our own storm and be a survivor. Perspective can help us do that.

In *Adversity* we talk about how to stop crying, how to feel hopeful again, how to cope with change and with things that can't be changed, and how to flourish anyway.

The Lord has given us the plan, the principles to live by, and opportunities to grow, but we grow through struggle as well as through joy. This is explained to us in the Doctrine and Covenants 29:39: "For if they never should have bitter they could not know the sweet." *Adversity* is about blessings in disguise.

Adversity is a book about all kinds of people struggling more or less successfully with all kinds of problems. And it is full of flooding proof of God's goodness.

Build thee more stately mansions, O my soul,
As the swift seasons roll!
Leave thy low-vaulted past!
Let each new temple, nobler than the last,
Shut thee from heaven with a dome more vast,
Till thou at length art free,
Leaving thine outgrown shell by life's unresting sea!

Oliver Wendell Holmes
"The Chambered Nautilus"

Introduction

A Look at Adversity

"Why a book about adversity?"

"Why not a happy book?"

"What gives you the right to speak out on this dour subject, anyway?"

Such have been the questions asked when I shared with others the subject of this book. My answers are simple.

First, I have written a book about adversity because it is something everybody is into these days. Or so it seems.

A book about adversity is important since perspective helps when we're struggling. Coping effectively with trouble by applying principles of the gospel to life's trying times is a God-given truth to live by. It makes great people, and the world needs great people. But not everybody is great under duress—at least not at first. When there is lack of understanding of lifesaving principles, big problems can grow from small ones. Hopefully a book like this can help stem the tide of error.

Second, as paradoxical as it may sound, this is really a book about happiness. Winter can prepare us for the loveliness of spring—prepare us to value it, as well. Trouble can heighten our sensitivity to things we might otherwise miss.

I believe that there is no such thing as a problem without a gift in its hands, and the gift is the kind that brings ultimate joy. We need more joy in the world, more lift to the spirit of man, more closeness with God.

Third, my right to speak out on this subject comes from experience. I, like you, have been there. Many, many times. And as a result I know some things that I didn't know before!

But there is more. I write of adversity because it can be inspiring. Over the years I have become aware of brave, gallant, undaunted people plagued by adversity in one form or another. I marvel at them. The refiner's fire can be so very good for people.

I recall being filled with a kind of wonder as a young girl when I read excerpts from the personal writings of Robert

Louis Stevenson. In my maturity I am even more impressed at Stevenson's courage and determination to overcome adversity. He wrote under the most trying conditions. He wrote chilled to the bone because he had only an unheated flat to live in. He wrote fevered with a dread disease. He wrote lying on his couch sickened with fever, weak with illness and hunger. He wrote wracked and retching. But he wrote! To Stevenson there simply was no other way. To give up was unthinkable to a man with purpose in life.

. Adversity in our own lives can bring life's purpose to mind.

Bad times have certain scientific value, according to Emerson. In his "Conduct of Life" essays he says that the trying times are occasions a good learner would not miss. One can learn a great deal. Can it be, then, that if one doesn't kick against the pricks, increased understanding comes—the nature of God, the importance of the adventure of life?

It would seem so.

Studying people who are struggling can be motivating. For example, there was a gentle, wholesome woman whose husband became involved in a financial scam. They were publicly disgraced and impoverished. How did she react? She kept her pleasant demeanor by pushing her inner strength into gear. She let no one know how deeply she was hurting. She took action, too, carrying two morning newspaper routes. She shared portions of her journal with me for that period. It included an accounting of the family finances which showed a steadily growing bank account from money made delivering papers before others were awake. Her conquering spirit heightened her self-esteem; newfound value within her brought a kind of happiness and a sense of well-being.

Small souls shrink with trouble, but great ones stretch above it.

There was the youth I knew who stoutly defended his alcoholic mother and devotedly shouldered additional burdens of family life in her stead. The father had long since fled the home. This young man scrounged for income and for time to do homework. He set youth aside. In the process he had to endure his mother's ugly and inappropriate abuse. But he doggedly did his duty. Time passed and he has grown into a distinguished and compassionate citizen.

There was the terminally ill single woman, deprived of the traditional fullness of life—marriage, children, professional service—who inevitably rose to the occasion. When visitors came to comfort her, they were the ones comforted. They left having been lifted and taught by her radiant faith and her accepting patience.

Patience is a heavenly virtue. Few need patience when the sun is shining and the breezes are mellow. However, when stress impacts a life, patience can be learned.

There was a dashing man whose wife developed a personality that to him was incredibly annoying and strident. As these traits surfaced over the years, he began to detest her and to hate his life with her. (And that may not be a strong enough description for what he felt!) To make matters worse, she was suddenly stricken with a debilitating disease—and she didn't die. She lived. She had to be cared for!

For the husband, life hadn't turned out the way he had planned. He had character beneath his sophistication, however, and he did not elect to abandon her with excuse. Rather, he learned to believe and behave like a man of God. He served her dutifully, sacrificing many important aspects of his own life. And as he applied God's principles with increasing understanding, love bloomed. He serves her now with generous love. She receives it with gratitude and an increased confidence about her own worth.

Oh, what I have learned from such people! Those who bear up under crushing burdens rob misfortune of its power.

How do they do it? Tried to their limit, tested where it hurts most, these people rise to choice levels. How do they keep from making bigger problems out of an original trial?

We will discuss this question later in the book.

Some people give in, close up, sob, and sulk. Some complain to one and all, wringing their hands in self-pity and decline.

We will talk about attitude—not to judge but to lend perspective.

Some troubles come unbidden and unannounced. Others we bring upon ourselves. This book points up the foolishness of looking about for someone else to hold responsible for what's happening. Some look for anyone, including God, to blame for their burdens. They seek a scapegoat for sin, grief, lack of fortitude, sagging morals, poor choices, disappointment, and persistent ignorance of the principles of the gospel and the value in living them.

One can learn, as well, from negative examples.

Thus, we can see the ballooning of burdens when we wallow in adversity or when we react without nobleness and wisdom, without God's guidance. This will only compound adversity. Often we reap the whirlwind, suffering more deeply than we might have in our season of testing.

We will present examples of adversity in this light in later chapters.

The purpose of this book, *Adversity,* is not to define the word. It is not to describe endless problems of life. You already know these things. The purpose is to share perspective about different kinds of people, different kinds of problems, and different ways people deal with these problems. We will consider the good that can come from the bad things in life. We hope to stir up a remembrance of blessings from Heavenly Father. And we will remind you of eternal principles, God-given, which can surface one day again when you need them most.

In *The Vicar of Wakefield* by Oliver Goldsmith, we learn this: "The greatest object in the universe is a good man struggling with adversity; yet there is still a greater, which is the good man that comes to relieve it." Many people need help in overcoming adversity. One purpose of this book is to stimulate good feelings and bright ideas, as well as a determination in the heart of the oppressed to live outside themselves in love and service to others; such living is an antidote to suffering and struggle.

Finally, it is our purpose to reverently but emphatically leave a testimony not only that God lives and loves but also that he cares! He is mindful of what is happening to us, of our heartaches and our frustrations and our hopelessness. Even if we have brought these things upon ourselves by our own sin or foolishness, he cares. The scriptures prove this. God knows our weaknesses. He counts on our strengths. He requires us to use our talents, experience, and example to bless his other children on earth. He waits to bless us in ways that won't impinge upon our free agency and personal growth.

Adversity can bring us closer to God in spirit. It can help us gradually become more like him.

In the stories related in the following chapters, some of the names have been changed and details altered to protect the privacy of the individuals involved, but the stories are based on fact. The heartbreak and the wrestle under pressure of severe problems has been valid in every case.

Some situations and their accompanying burdens are more life-threatening or deeply serious than others mentioned. Some examples may seem too lightweight to be included in a book titled *Adversity.* Some are about troubles people bring on themselves. They are included because people are at different levels of learning, and upon one strength another is given. Line upon line we learn.

The principles of the gospel of Jesus Christ are implicit in the examples.

Jesus endured the mighty testings in all aspects of life. He was "tempted of Satan" in the wilderness, and he resisted. Then "Jesus returned in the power of the Spirit" (Luke 4:14). This, it seems to me, is the pattern of our own adversity. We will be tried in a variety of ways. If we meet these demands in strength according to God's will and his example, we, too, will come forth in the power of the Spirit. As he was proven, we can be.

Because the Savior had real life experiences, he understands. He hungered when he fasted forty days in the wilderness. He was attacked, both verbally and physically. He was rejected and was eventually betrayed by one of his chosen associates. He knows! He knows! That should comfort us.

Our ultimate goal is to be like him so that we may dwell in the presence of God throughout all eternity. And meanwhile, we'll know inner joy and greater peace as we push through the problems of this life. Thus, we should welcome opportunities to learn and to show greater devotion to his will and the will of the Father.

Solving our problems according to the principles of the gospel and in the attitude of a contrite spirit is a certain way of building what Oliver Wendell Holmes described as "more stately mansions" of our soul. Hence the symbol of the nautilus shell used throughout this book.

I am grateful to the Lord for his unfailing support, for his love, and for the saving principles of the gospel. I am grateful, too, beyond adequate expression, for the comfort and the gifts of the Holy Ghost.

I am indebted, as well, to the people who have helped me in particular ways, in particular times with my struggles. Aren't you?

Perhaps, after all, that is the second major thrust of this book (the first being our own goal of learning to cope appropriately with inevitable adversity)—to be effectively useful when someone else is suffering.

Understanding the struggle, finding answers to the questions about life and God that trouble introduces, is impetus to personal progress. Being quick to appropriately meet the need of others about us who suffer is to emulate the Savior.

Unless we consider that life is school and there are things for us to learn not only about behaving ourselves in times of happiness but also about the need for obedience, unless we seek to understand the critical benefits of obeying gospel principles—unless we do these things we can bring adversity upon ourselves.

We can needlessly turn choice blessings such as health, peace, family unity, and personal honor into burdens of physical weakness, guilty conscience, divorce, financial disaster, and estrangement from God.

Take a hard look at
those things which we
needlessly turn into
burdens
when they were meant
to be blessings.

1

How to Turn Blessings Into Burdens

Nobody really wants to make trouble for himself or herself. Sometimes, however, that is exactly what we do—we turn blessings into burdens through our actions and attitudes.

Here are eighteen ways we can turn rich blessings into dreadful burdens. Of course there are other ways, but consider these for a moment.

1. Sin.
2. Don't repent, recoup, make restitution.
3. Live without prayer.
4. Think you know more than Church leaders—or parents, experts, even God.
5. Be casual about sacred ordinances.
6. Fail to read your patriarchal blessing frequently.
7. Withhold love.
8. Hold a grudge; be unforgiving.
9. Fail to ask forgiveness.
10. Be arrogant, full of pride.
11. Think of self first—what's in it for me?
12. Assume that you can get something for nothing.
13. Assume that no one will ever know.
14. Complain.

15. Be ungrateful; count your troubles instead of bless-
    ings.
16. Ignore scripture study.
17. Be lazy, manufacturing excuses, ignoring oppor-
    tunities.
18. Break the Ten Commandments. (Look them over
    again, just in case you've forgotten the one about the
    Sabbath day or honoring parents or lying, cheating,
    adultery, etc.)

Look to your habits and attitudes. Look to your responses
to situations. Don't choose to be a problem. Be a problem
solver. Be a burden lifter. Value the word of God and the place
of God in your life.

To err is human, but to make unnecessary mistakes in life is
not smart. One might even suggest that it is stupid. Surely it
can be painful. It is how to turn blessings into burdens.

To take a perfectly good blessing and turn it into a burden
through sin or stupidity is courting trouble. One might even
call such a course self-imposed adversity. Ignorance of the law
or disobedience of fine principles promises problems. And
who needs burdens when we could have had blessings?

Consider this simple example: One day I was making a cake
to use as a visual aid in a meeting. A committee had a task to
perform, and I wanted to show that with proper planning it
would be easy—a "piece of cake" as the saying goes.

I arose early and attacked the project with virtuous en-
thusiasm. I would make the biggest and best cake I had ever
produced—a six egg cake, light as down and delicious to eat.
Just as I began breaking the eggs into the mixture, the tele-
phone rang. The call from the East Coast person in a state of
trauma was made according to her time zone and not mine. I
listened while I went on with the cake because I was feeling
the scrunch of time to finish my visual aid.

It would have been better if I had stopped the mixing
altogether. In my concern for the caller, my brain short-
circuited. I began tossing egg shells into the mix and eggs into
the sink. This fact did not become clear to me until the cake
was baked. It was not the lightest cake ever, and there were
crunchy shells where one least expected them to be.

I used the cake as a visual aid, all right, but I made a point different from the "piece of cake" idea. I used the cake failure to show how something very nice can become awful when we are not in control, when we don't think through to the result of certain action, when we don't consider that what we are doing is different from what we ought to be doing, and when what we are doing brings disappointment—even trouble.

Here are some scriptures to study that reinforce the idea that we can turn blessings into burdens of our own making:

> Inasmuch as you are found transgressors, you cannot escape my wrath in your lives.
>
> Inasmuch as ye are cut off for transgression, ye cannot escape the buffetings of Satan until the day of redemption. (D&C 104:8–9.)

I remember when someone I loved was cut off from the Church. A friend called with a comfort and a warning: "It will be worse yet, for a time, while the buffetings of Satan invoke real trouble. I know. I watched it with my own wife. After her excommunication the buffetings of Satan became real and terrible. Christ supports us but Satan tosses us about when we step into his arena. If people knew this, they'd stay far away from sin."

It proved true.

> And without the ordinances thereof, and the authority of the priesthood, the power of godliness is not manifest unto men in the flesh;
>
> For without this no man can see the face of God (D&C 84:21–22).

I recall a missionary who had sinned, confessed to his mission president, and been sent home dishonorably discharged. He came directly from the airplane to our house. We had watched this neighbor grow up and struggle only to make repeated fresh resolves. His wail when he fell into my arms weeping was, "If I couldn't make it as a set-apart missionary, how will I ever make it now without such support?"

And what a battle he has had—he who turned his priesthood-supported blessings into burdens has a difficult battle turning burdens back into blessings. Good advice is given in section 10 of the Doctrine and Covenants.

Pray always, that you may come off conqueror; yea, that you may conquer Satan, and that you may escape the hands of the servants of Satan that do uphold his work. Behold, they have sought to destroy you. (D&C 10:5–6.)

There was a priesthood leader who admitted that he was unprepared for the intensity of the drive within himself to get wealth, to prove to his peers that he could "make it big." He didn't consider that his actions were not in hand with gospel principles and commandments of God. The man lost balance and the modifying influence of being involved in the gospel because he was immersed in the scramble for wealth, at any price. He now has time in prison to think about the way he turned his blessings of home and family and respectability into the burdens of confinement and shame.

The more wicked part of the Nephites were destroyed.

For the Lord would not suffer, after he had led them out of the land of Jerusalem and kept and preserved them from falling into the hands of their enemies, yea, he would not suffer that the words should not be verified, which he spake unto our fathers, saying that: *Inasmuch as ye will not keep my commandments ye shall not prosper in the land.*

Wherefore, the Lord did visit them in great judgment; nevertheless, he did spare the righteous that they should not perish, but did deliver them out of the hands of their enemies. (Omni 1:5–7; italics added.)

This reference is a jewel of an example of people who manage to turn their blessings into burdens. Such action brings terrible adversity.

Why look for trouble? Why bring it on ourselves when we have our hands full with life already?

In considering adversity in our lives, in daring to take a deep look at misery, we learn that God's principles help us deal with everyday challenges and temptations. Knowing how to walk in wisdom's paths is necessary for the successful, fruitful living of which adversity is part.

In Helaman 12 is an outpouring worth reading again: "O how foolish, and how vain, and how evil, and devilish, and how quick to do iniquity, and how slow to do good, are the children of men; yea, how quick to hearken unto the words of the evil one, and to set their hearts upon the vain things of the world!

"Yea, how quick to be lifted up in pride; yea, how quick to boast, and do all manner of that which is iniquity; and how slow are they to remember the Lord their God, and to give ear unto his counsels, yea, how slow to walk in wisdom's paths!

"Behold, they do not desire that the Lord their God, who hath created them, should rule and reign over them; notwithstanding his great goodness and his mercy towards them, they do set at naught his counsels, and they will not that he should be their guide." (Helaman 12:4–6.)

Now, that is a sermon of worth! The negative attitude it describes is the essence of how blessings get turned into burdens.

Since we are not perfect and we are forced to interact in life with others who are not perfect, and since we have a moral purpose to use our talents to avoid self-imposed adversity, let us get on with the challenge.

Hopefully we'll do better in the future with the blessings God has given us so abundantly. Hope is a positive attitude and a powerful, pushing force. It is the opposite of despair. Let us hope, and let us move forward.

Elder Marion D. Hanks once told a group of students not to let the sorrows that inevitably result from sin disqualify them from their blessings or contributions. He said, "Don't shrivel inside when you hear the pointed sermon or lesson; don't turn from the brotherhood of the Saints or the path of the Lord because you have made some mistakes. Don't give up and die spiritually. Christ suffered 'these things' that we might *not* eternally suffer, on condition of our repentance."

The great wonder of the gospel of Jesus Christ—a wonder that much of the world doesn't understand—is that heartbreak and misery *can be assuaged* through Christ. Also, he will help us become what in our hearts we want to be—as he is. With God nothing is impossible. That is a good thing to keep in mind.

The Lord has told us to watch and pray always. He comforts us, saying that if we will draw near to him, he will draw near to us. The experiment should be ours. It can protect us from turning our blessings into burdens.

My personal witness, my experience with agony of soul, with blessed relief, and with growth is that he is there for us.

I have seen countless reenactments of the prodigal who at last turns homeward toward the father who rushes forth to meet him. Heavenly Father will do this for us if we turn to him and seek his help as well as his forgiveness.

Ours is the mission to keep from turning blessings into burdens. We need daily refreshment of the Spirit and firm resolve to keep from breaking God's commandments and thus turning blessings into burdens. When repentance and change come into the life of the sinner, when God's principles are applied to trying situations, blessings pour from heaven.

I recommend pursuing truth and seeking heavenly help so that we may live life with serenity, faith, and positive outcome of the trials, temptations, and despair along the way.

It has been said in the scriptures, sung in the hymns, and written in the volumes of wise men that "sweet are the uses of adversity."

How can this be? Adversity—who needs it?

We are here on earth
to be proven,
here on earth to endure
until we are safely dead.

2

Adversity—
Who Needs It?

"Why me?" the young, new widow moaned.

"Why not!" the cripple cried, certain that trouble was meant not only for a select few. Who did the lady think she was that she should be spared suffering?

The same is true for each of us when we might be inclined to feel we're different from the rest of God's children.

"Why me?" Why not, indeed. It's part of the plan.

Trial comes in different ways at different stages in life. But whatever trouble it is and whenever it comes, when it is your problem, it is painful.

There was the teenager, for example, who complained to her twin brother about the blows life had dealt her. She said to him, "It isn't fair. It absolutely isn't fair. You got curly hair and a straight nose."

He was a good brother and wanted to help his sister in the unique way brothers often have. He answered, "Right. But think of it this way—you got the straight hair and the curly nose."

Straight hair and a curly nose at one stage in life may be a dreadful way to suffer, but things can get worse.

Why are we tried? Why adversity? Who needs it?

Apparently everyone does.

We are here on earth to be proven, here on earth to endure. Through adversity we gain valuable experience and understanding about life, principles, and the nature of God and his children. Adversity can mellow us and prepare us to draw closer to God.

Adversity proves whom God can trust.

Adversity gives us experience.

Adversity brings us closer to the Lord.

One day I was walking to work and had stopped for a traffic light. There was a strong wind whipping around the buildings. A teenage boy suddenly moved past me as I stood on the curb. He stepped into the traffic pattern, which was heavy so close to town at that hour of the day. Startled, I reached out to stop him. It was then that I realized he wasn't just a carefree youth; he was blind!

He was on his way to the blind center a block or two further on. We walked that way together, friends now, as he said, since I had saved his life.

He explained that at the blind school he was taught to listen to the traffic pattern before he crossed a street. However, the wind that day was so severe that he couldn't hear properly, and he'd decided to take a chance. He was grateful that I was watching.

I asked him how long he'd been blind. He told me this story.

"When I was eight years old my sole purpose in life was to be the world's best and most famous baseball player," explained Glenn. "I was practicing one afternoon when a fellow player threw the bat after a hit. It landed across my eyes. This accident brought a terrible period of tribulation for my entire family.

"I was a mess," Glenn said. "I lived, but there was nothing science could do to restore my sight."

"What happened next?" I asked, intensely interested in this vigorous, handsome teenager's story.

"I withdrew from life. I sulked. I had tantrums. I wouldn't go to school. I wouldn't talk to friends. I hated my family, and I especially cried out in anger against God. I mean vocally. I would shout my hate—much to my religious mother's deep distress. This went on for many months. One day my father coaxed me into going outside with him to fly a kite. He said I'd be able to feel the tug on the kite. It would be exhilarating, even if I couldn't see it.

"We got the kite up, and I was feeling pretty good as I held the string and felt the force at work. Suddenly, the course of the breeze changed and the kite got caught in a tree.

"I was soon out of control. I screamed and lay down on the grass and kicked. Oh, I was one ugly kid. My father called for the fire department, in desperation, I guess. They came and got the kite down, but it was broken. More tantrums from me.

" 'Fix it! Fix it!' I screamed. My dad tried explaining it all to me, but I would not be comforted. It was just another of life's rotten tricks. Then Dad took my hand and moving my fingers with his, we traced the broken crossbars of the flimsy kite.

" 'See, son,' he said. 'It is broken. It can't be fixed. Any Band-Aid work, however carefully done, would add weight to the kite and it wouldn't fly. It just can't be fixed. Like your eyes! We'll have to go and do something else.' "

The young man paused in his tracks, shook his head, remembering. Then he turned toward me and said, "That was the phrase that made the difference. 'Go and do something else.' God had given us a lot of options and Dad would find another one for us. I'm going to the blind school now and learning a trade."

His feet had felt the pebbles laid in the concrete in front of the school as a signal for the blind people.

"I'm here," he explained confidently. "Thanks again. Make it a good day."

He didn't say "Have a good day" as so many well-wishers do. He said, "*Make* it a good day."

With all that we have going for us, why not make it a good day? A positive approach is the beginning of winning.

One certainty is that neither here nor hereafter are we suddenly going to emerge with good qualities of character unless we have developed them. We won't reach the level of celestial living if we have not prepared ourselves.

Adversity is a vital part of this preparation for at least three reasons:

1. Adversity proves whom God can trust. Who of us, as Job did, will stand firm, be obedient under all circumstances, and love God no matter what comes into our lives?

2. Adversity, well-handled, can increase our understanding and compassion. When we have survived the refiner's fire, we are experienced in ways that make us more effective in meeting the needs of others. We learn through adversity.

3. Adversity can bring us closer to God. When we are in deep need, prayers usually are more fervent and more frequent.

If we had everything we wanted and needed without asking of Heavenly Father, we would lose sight of the hand of God in our lives.

The most trying circumstances can become worth it somehow, when considered as unique schooling to bring us wisdom, to prove our trustworthiness and our love of God, and to quicken our compassion toward the plight of others.

Who needs adversity? Everyone. It's part of the plan. It is "God designed" for the well-being and development of his children. It is wise, then, to meet the test of adversity with success.

A classic story of meeting adversity with a winning attitude is the account of the burning of Thomas A. Edison's laboratories. A spontaneous explosion occurred and others quickly spread, in dramatic repetition of the first burst, moving across the film processing plant through freight cars and on to ignite alcohol storage tanks that sent fantastic towers of flames into the air.

Water pressure failed, and the fire was soon out of control. It was a spectacular fire! Edison sent for his wife, telling her to bring her friends because they'd never see anything like this fire again.

Later, when Edison surveyed the blackened ruins of a lifetime of effort, he turned to his discouraged associates and said, "You can always make capital out of disaster. Now we are rid of a lot of our past mistakes."

He was sixty-seven at the time and began rebuilding the plant before the last ember was finally subdued on the old ruin.

He could have given up. Instead he proved that youth doesn't have the only handle on growth and that preachers aren't the only people who understand hope. Besides, if adversity helps us get rid of past mistakes, *we need it*!

Each person, young and old, must rise or fall to the challenges of his or her life. How we respond to them helps us rapidly become what, at last, we are going to be.

Pleasant or miserable times can be tools for learning if our attitude is appropriate. Attitude in adversity particularly can help turn the hopeless into the hopeful.

God is good and all-powerful, and yet up and down the streets of life there is untold suffering, struggle, frustration, wickedness, deprivation, heartbreak, and more. Why?

Some troubles we bring upon ourselves. Some we have no control over. We can only endure, cope, resolve, and learn from them. But what is God's purpose for us in all this? Let's refer to the word of God for understanding.

There was a conversation in heaven regarding the plan of life, as reported in Abraham 3:24–26: ". . . and we will make an earth whereon these may dwell; and we will prove them herewith, to see if they will do all things whatsoever the Lord their God shall command them; and they who keep their first estate shall be added upon; and they who keep not their first estate shall not have glory in the same kingdom with those who keep their first estate; and they who keep their second estate shall have glory added upon their heads for ever and ever."

That's the plan. It is our understanding that in the world before this one we all heard this plan of life presented. We had a choice of whether we wanted to be part of the experience such a plan provided.

How precious the experience must have appeared to us then! How powerful the promises! All of us who are here on earth voted to come. We had our agency, and we agreed that no matter what life might offer us in the fine details, no matter what we might have to suffer in learning and growing, we wanted to be part of it. We voted to take a body and go for the testing, the learning.

Although we probably didn't envision the details of the

daily grind, to me our decision to come to earth meant that we might have said something like one of these:

"I will go down and suffer a learning disability."

"I will endure a frustrating marriage."

"I'll take up my life in loneliness."

"I will live life working hard all my years without success."

"I will be the victim of a terrible scam or the object of abuse."

Whatever challenges we were to face, nevertheless we wanted to go down and have a remarkable experience.

Great leaders of the Church of Jesus Christ have always encouraged people to come to grips with the purpose of life. Understanding our purpose can help us face suffering and sacrifice, and can turn them to our benefit.

In speaking of this matter, President Joseph F. Smith said that the purpose of our mortal existence is to see if, through temptations, trials, and tribulations, a person can maintain a faithful demeanor and prove worthy of exaltation in the kingdom of God. Said President Smith, "If for us this were the last moment of existence, it would mean little or nothing. . . . Life is dear to us now because it will always be dear to us, even as long as time shall last—and beyond, where the days are no longer numbered and where the sweep of the years is measured only by the endlessness of things to come."

D. H. Wells suggested that we have to pass through an earthly probation in order to prove whether we will be faithful to our trust, our integrity, and our God. If people will do this important thing, they can "come forth in the resurrection clothed upon with immortality and eternal lives." (In *Journal of Discourses*, 12:136.)

President Ezra Taft Benson has taught us the importance of free agency in the life of each of God's children. It has been an on-going emphasis in all his teachings. He said this about the importance of choices in life. *"This life is a probation—a probation in which you and I prove our mettle.* A probation that has eternal consequences for each of us. And now is our time and season—as every generation has had theirs—to learn our duties and to do them.

"The Lord has so arranged things in this life that men are free agents unto themselves—to do good or evil." (*An Enemy Hath Done This* [Salt Lake City: Parliament Publishers, 1969], pp. 53–54.)

This grand adventure of choosing well is at every stage worth the battle. We are here to learn what the Savior learned. God is the author of the format, and he is the master teacher. He will not deny us our right to learn for ourselves those lessons that will prove us herewith, that will mark our development. This development includes how we deal with what happens to us, how we feel about life and God, and how much we learn that is of value to us now and in the eternities.

Life is a very special kind of schooling. It is a training ground for our next estate. When we become converted to—not just convinced of—that truth and idea, our trials and tribulations will be more meaningful to us.

Adversity—who needs it? Everyone. Adversity is part of God's plan. In the remainder of the book we'll discuss adversity in terms of its effect upon our lives. After all, if we are going to have to go through adversity, knowing what's in it for us may help.

This is the challenge of life:
To see how much we can endure
of defeat and heartbreak
and still come forth
with our faith intact.

3

Adversity Proves Whom God Can Trust

Adversity proves whom God can trust. Who of us, as Job did, will stand firm, be obedient, and love God no matter what comes into our lives? We are proven through adversity.

A few years ago I was talking with some people of Rexburg, Idaho, about the devastating flood following the bursting of the Teton Dam.

The story of one woman is especially interesting in terms of this chapter's focus. I asked this woman if her family had been seriously affected by the flood. She drove me to a hill overlooking the city to which citizens had rushed when the flood warning was given. From there they could watch the wide path of raging water and follow the destruction of their own homes in its wake.

"Yes," she exclaimed, "we were seriously affected. But first let me give you some background."

Then she told me that the family had struggled for years to get adequate housing for their growing family. At last there came a day when a fine house was finished with appropriate bedrooms and storage. They had worked out a remarkable facility for their year's supply of food and commodities.

One morning shortly before dawn broke, they smelled smoke. Their new home on rural acreage was consumed by flames. The fire took everything but their lives and the night clothing they were wearing. Everything—including the food storage gathered at the counsel of a prophet.

"But, Sister Cannon, it was wonderful to see the Lord's blessings unfold," she continued. "Before the day was over we had clothes to wear and places to sleep with neighbors. Within a year we were able to build another house and fill it with our children and our newly acquired year's supply of staples."

"That is wonderful," I agreed.

"Yes, but shortly after we moved in the Teton Dam broke. We were right in the path of that raging mile-wide broom that swept this valley clean. From this hill where we stand, we watched our house go. We had binoculars, but because we were crying they weren't much good."

A neighbor who didn't understand gospel principles had scoffed at this family's futile preparations for some future time. When trouble came, their food storage had burned or washed away. Now that neighbor said to the family, "What good is it to collect all that food storage, all those emergency supplies? If you go through that ridiculous process again, that is your business, but don't tell me about it. It hasn't done you any good. Why go to that trouble if you can't eat it when you need it?"

My friend was thoughtful before such an accusation. Then she firmly replied, "Nobody told me I had to eat it."

And she is right; she had been told only to store it, and she had been obedient. In spite of adversity her spirit was sweet.

I thought of Joseph Smith's response to trouble during a certain period of his life. It was 1842, just two years before he was murdered by his enemies. He was in hiding and wrote:

> And as for the perils which I am called to pass through, they seem but a small thing to me, as the envy and wrath of man have been my common lot all the days of my life; . . . God knoweth all these things. . . . Deep water is what I am wont to swim in. It all has become a second nature to me; and I feel, like Paul, to glory in tribulation; for to this day has the God of my fathers delivered me out of them all, and will deliver me from henceforth; for behold, and lo, I shall triumph over all my enemies, for the Lord God hath spoken it. (D&C 127:2.)

Like Joseph we can triumph over our enemies, surmount our problems. We can do it with God's help.

The Lord has told us that if we can be trusted to behave like Saints and disciples using wisdom, all will be well with us. In the Doctrine and Covenants 112:13 we read his words, "And after their temptations, and much tribulation, behold I, the Lord, will feel after them, and if they harden not their hearts, and stiffen not their necks against me . . . I will heal them."

Following a church assignment I filled in Wyoming, a woman asked if she could talk with me for a few minutes alone. She didn't want to brag or to be inappropriate in any way by sharing a personal experience. She wanted only to testify of the goodness of God to his children in trouble, and she wanted me to listen to her for a moment. She gave me permission to use her story.

This family had always enjoyed a large vegetable garden. The father loved to till the earth. Repeatedly, from planting through harvest, he pronounced that it was good for a man's soul as well as his stomach to prepare the soil and nurture the seedlings into a delicious crop of produce.

Then there would come a morning when Dad would go through the house calling, "Harvest time!" And the family would laughingly race each other to the strawberry patch, the pea vines, or the corn stalks to find the first ripe offerings of each crop.

It had been hard work squeezed into very busy lives of family members, but on each succeeding time of harvest, it was all worth it. Dad had taught them well.

Suddenly, their happy world crumbled. In many ways trouble heaped upon trouble. The father was critically injured in an explosion at his place of employment. He lived, but it would be many long months before he could work again. A married child was having troubles and desperate for ongoing help. The young family members needed security and guidance. The mother's strength was running thin as she tried to juggle driving long hours back and forth to be by her husband's hospital bed, and meeting the needs of other family members, plus keeping up on household chores.

At last Dad came home—but so did a grandchild. Each of them needed an incredible amount of care. There wasn't time for work outside. The ploughed field sprouted June grass where vegetables used to be. The woman apologized to her husband for failing him in this way. She sighed, "There will be no garden this year."

Ten-year-old Matt was listening. "But we must have a garden, Mother! You heard President Kimball at conference. He said everybody should have a garden. He is the prophet! We must have a garden."

"The child was the teacher of the parent," my new friend continued. "And though it was weeks late for planting a crop, I knew we had to try."

They soaked the seeds in warm water before placing them in the ground. And they prayed in family circle over the planting, over the fields, and over the elements of nature, as well as for the father's health and the well-being of the family struggling with so many problems.

That year the good weather lasted longer than usual—long enough for the crops to mature.

One morning late in the season, the family was awakened by a joyful father calling, "Harvest time!"

And it was a harvest time, for produce they sorely needed for the winter ahead and for the blessings they had received from Heavenly Father in answer to fervent prayer.

This fine family proved that they would be valiant and follow the word of God and the counsel of his prophet even in times of terrible hardship. These people are witnesses that the Lord will help with our burdens if we try to do what we are supposed to do.

Whom can God trust? Who will suffer appropriately in order to learn the lessons, be the example of a believer and a witness to the hand of God in the affairs of man? Who will endure trials to help in the work of the kingdom of God on earth?

During the mid-seventies the Church membership expanded rapidly across eastern Canada to the state of New York. There was an amazing ethnic mix of people living in that area, people with many different kinds of needs and problems. One of the most pressing needs was church buildings close to where the people lived. They needed easy access to church training and programs, and they needed guidance. They needed buildings to welcome new members and investigators.

Rented halls of various kinds and some public school buildings were the norm, but they didn't promote a good image of the Church and its converts, nor did they allow the full Church program.

The stake president was certain that before the stake could grow sufficiently to multiply into other stakes and to shrink the far-flung boundaries, there had to be suitable buildings erected and dedicated. He initiated a five-year plan for this goal.

It was too slow. People didn't respond.

So the stake president decided to test the people with a crash cash effort to fund at least some building in a short time. It was a courageous move—doomed to failure some said when consideration was given to the period of inflation they were in and the financial burdens on the people.

According to the stake president the Spirit moved him mightily. There was no other choice. They had to try!

As he prepared for the stake gathering at which the challenge would be issued, he felt impressed to bestow, through the power of the priesthood, a blessing with a promise upon the members of that stake in this undertaking.

People had been asked to fast and pray—to prepare themselves before coming to this conference. The people felt the Spirit of the Lord in that meeting as the stake president pronounced a special blessing upon them. If they would labor diligently to meet this crisis, the Lord would indeed pour out his blessings upon them. He would help them. They would be able to meet their obligations and contribute to the building program.

So it was said. So it was fulfilled. Later, many reports proved the remarkable blessings from heaven that came as people prayed for help in meeting the need.

One man, for example, was closing his business because times were hard. After prayer he suddenly received an idea to improve it. He followed the prompting and sales rose to a record volume. He could pay his part for the building fund, and more, if need be.

Another man's struggle to meet the assessment included fervent prayer on his knees by his office chair. The idea came to him afterwards that he should ask for a raise to cover the amount he needed above his own resources to respond to the stake president's challenge. He asked for that amount. It was given to him with a retroactive clause! He was able to pay the full amount of his obligation sooner than he might otherwise have been able to.

It was a wonderful spiritual awakening for the members in that area. It was a strengthening time as the unfolding of little miracles happened in numerous families. People without work got work; seemingly worthless investments became profitable; forgotten bank accounts came to light; creative ideas that were remunerative flourished.

People who proved that God could trust them were blessed, and they met the stake's financial goal. Within three short years three stakes were made from that original one. More than buildings or numbers resulted from this period of sacrifice and struggle—people grew.

On the other hand, the study of the scriptures teaches us that if we do not take adversity as a person of faith should, it will not be well with us. We will be in Satan's arena. Life is full of evidence to support this.

What is trust? What does it mean to be trustworthy under the weight of temptation, the burdens of illness, poverty, misunderstanding, disappointment, loneliness, handicap, heartbreak, persecution?

From life itself we can draw a comparison. We use trust every day. It is critical to life. It is illustrated in the case of the loving parent who hires a baby-sitter. It is seen in the case of the owner who leaves a new clerk to mind the store. It is evidenced every time we mail a precious package for a loved one.

Trust implies responsibility, dependability, accountability, stability, honesty, commitment. Webster defines trust as faith.

When we understand the glorious work of God and our place in it, these examples might seem too simplistic. Yet, they help us realize that trust is imperative to order and progress, as well as to peace of mind.

Remember, God's work is to bring to pass the immortality

and eternal life of man. Our work is to help the Lord with his work. Doing this work is imperative to our personal joy.

Now, the devil's work is to try and thwart the Lord's work. And at this moment the old and stirring hymn comes to mind, "Who's on the Lord's Side?" (*Hymns,* 1985, no. 260).

In April 1830, when the Church was again organized according to God's will, instructions from God were given as to the duties of leadership and the duties of members. Among other sacred guidance, this counsel was given: "There is a possibility that man may fall from grace and depart from the living God; therefore let the church take heed and pray always, lest they fall into temptation" (D&C 20:32–33).

Also, elders and priests were counseled that God's children are to be taught all things concerning the Church "to their understanding, previous to their partaking of the sacrament. . . . And the members shall manifest before the church, and also before the elders, by a godly walk and conversation, that they are worthy of it, that there may be works and faith agreeable to the holy scriptures—walking in holiness before the Lord." (D&C 20:68–69.)

This is powerful instruction to dwell upon when trouble hits us. We are to respond as one with faith agreeable to the holy word and way of the Lord.

Recently I sat in sacrament service and pondered the sacrifice of Jesus. I wondered, too, about the bitter cup my husband and I had been pressed into taking lately. It was little compared to the cup of our Lord, but we had struggled and suffered, fasted, prayed, waited. No answer. There were the despair, the tears, the sleepless nights with pacing and praying, the scripture study, the striving for patience. There were times of counseling together as well as listening to others who had endured similar heart-ripping trauma. Finally, when the resolution of a trial, a test, came, we were grateful that we had survived the traumatic time with our faith intact. In fact we were filled with a new closeness to God. On this particular day I took the sacrament in humility and gratitude for his suffering for us. How good God is. We had felt his sustaining presence even while he *allowed* us to go through an ordeal in order for us to grow. I was thankful as well that we hadn't made a bigger problem for ourselves by not being trustworthy. Giving up, complaining in self-pity, questioning—in any way turning away from God is not appropriate for one who has made sacred covenants!

I took the sacrament that day with a new commitment to the Lord's work, to the plan and the principles. In spite of—perhaps even because of—sadness and agony in trial, I could praise God.

Struggle proves the presence, the reality of Christ, his mission, and his sacrifice for us. Surely, with such a gift to us we should be trustworthy before God.

God will help us in a variety of ways. He has told us that by doing the things that we are supposed to do when we are supposed to do them, the "gates of hell shall not prevail against you; yea, and the Lord God will disperse the powers of darkness from before you, and cause the heavens to shake for your good" (D&C 21:6).

The gospel is more than a system of ethics. It is doing—experimenting upon the word, living according to God's way and his will. That means all the time, in good times and bad times alike. It means working with increasing effectiveness to keep from bringing trouble upon ourselves by not living the gospel, by turning blessings into burdens.

But however trials come, all of them can give us experience and be for our eternal good.

Neither here nor hereafter
are we suddenly going to emerge
with qualities of character
and a level of living
for which we have not prepared
ourselves.

4

Adversity Gives Us Experience

Adversity, well-handled, can increase our understanding and compassion. When we have survived the refiner's fire, we are experienced in ways that help us to be more effective in meeting the needs of others. We learn through adversity.

"These things shall give you experience" (D&C 122:7), the loving Lord reminds us. He knows what is good for us. He knows what help his children need. He can use us to help—and with experience we'll be more effective in service.

Adversity gives us experience. If we cope with it according to God's principles, we will find the blessings in the burdens.

It was Christmas Day 1973. Our family stood in the midst of affliction with a beloved young family member who had just learned that she suffered a terminal illness. There was nothing medical science could do.

Christine was the mother of three very small sons. President Harold B. Lee was counseling with her and with us.

President Lee said to her in comfort, "Don't worry. When the Lord wants you he'll take you. And it will be all right." Looking back upon this experience, his words seem ironic because President Lee died the next day. The young mother lived for another year. But in that conversation in the Lee home a prophet of God explained powerful principles that helped us all understand "Why me?" "Why this experience?" "Why now?" "Whatever for?" President Lee spoke of faith in God's power to perform miracles. He spoke of comfort and the peace that God could give to us if the desired miracles didn't happen. He asked our daughter-in-law if she would be willing to go through whatever was put before her, according to God's will, so that many people could learn important lessons.

In other words, would she be willing to lay down her life for others—as Christ did? That was the implication.

Her positive response was almost tentatively given. This beautiful young mother was so hopeful about being a good wife and mother. She had dreams . . . It was difficult in the extreme to admit willingness to submit to dying, if that was the will of God.

President Lee was gentle and thoughtful as he accepted her quiet, tearful answer.

Then he said soberly, "There is so much work to do. This people is just beginning to be tested. When you are a golden nugget, prepare for the refiner's fire! Now, go home; live each day that you have according to God's will. Nothing can ultimately hurt you then."

It put a new dimension on our trouble. It fired a new resolve to keep the commandments.

Sometimes in fast and testimony meeting people will stand and share stories of miracles. For example, one person might witness that 'their soldier son lived a clean life, and so he was spared, as were the sons of Helaman.' And there on the next row might sit the family of a son who also lived the clean life— yet he was not spared! Did this mean God didn't love that son, his family?

In the case of Christine, she had had the best of medical help, and she had received spiritual help from President Lee. She had not given offense to the Lord in her brief life. All the family fasted, prayed, and got their lives in order. We increased our offerings and our service. There had been priesthood blessings and a crying out in faith enough to move mountains. There was her patriarchal blessing promising a long life.

Notwithstanding, Christine died.

She was honored with a beautiful funeral service. The stake center overflowed with loving, caring, questioning people. Her young husband—our son—was chief mourner and a speaker, too. He was a great example of a believer and of one who had learned what he was supposed to learn from the trial of losing a beloved spouse.

This heartbroken husband admitted that things hadn't turned out the way he and Christine had wanted them to. But he was speaking at her funeral because it was her last request that he share their sure knowledge that God lives and loves them. This they had learned through their ordeal. It was all right. He testified of this.

It wasn't the broken heart that took center stage—difficult as this time was. It was the power and comfort of God pouring out new light and understanding upon those he loves and those whom he can use to accomplish much good among others of his children.

A lot of people did learn many lessons—as President Lee suggested. After the funeral, our son was repeatedly called upon to talk with people similarly tested. He could comfort with a keen compassion. He could point a way for flourishing under heartbreak. He could testify that principles applied to a problem bring forth the spirit, strength, and a sense of rightness. Such is the goodness of God.

It is suggested in this book that adversity can prove whom God can trust, who will love him anyway. Adversity can also give us experience that will be useful as we try to be of service in the Lord's work.

There are so many who need help.

Adversity can be an effective teacher. When we have a testimony of the gospel—even a flickering one—we are more likely to apply eternal principles to situations; then trouble can become a blessing.

Freedom of choice in how we will react to adversity is essential to existence and to progression. When the testing is tough, faith in God's goodness may be all there is to go on for a time. But then, as we are reminded in 2 Nephi 2:2, "Thou knowest the greatness of God; and he shall consecrate thine afflictions for thy gain."

We can learn from trial. We can slug it out, live it through, or wait in patience until we find the principle God has given to help us meet such a test and to gain great experience from it.

There is a powerful promise from God recorded in Doctrine and Covenants 122 upon which I based the following lines:

> If the heavens gather blackness,
> If the jaws of hell gape wide,
> If the gaze of loved ones lowers,
> If old friends now stand aside,
>
> If your shining dreams have vanished
> And your efforts seem in vain,
> O keep faithful, hopeful, patient.
> Rise above despair, disdain!
>
> With God's help you can survive this—
> Even flourish when you're tried.
> Life is school, life is learning.
> Count your blessings and abide.

Being content with mediocrity is not good enough for a disciple of Christ. Adversity can hone, polish, enlarge the soul, and even though such learning is hard, it can make us useful in the kingdom.

Life is no respecter of persons. Trouble will come when it will come. We do not know the Lord's particular schedule for our learning and our contribution. We do not know how our life might impact someone else's learning and contribution.

Life is suffering.

Buddha knew that life was suffering. The first of his four noble truths was that life is, indeed, suffering.

The Bible reminds us in its first pages that, thanks to Adam and Eve, we are really in for it. We must earn our bread by the sweat of the brow. We must bring forth children in pain. Now, if people are doing much reading about the rules of the plan of life—doing scripture study, that is—how have the details of the struggle so quickly escaped them? Such forgetting or ignoring brings the cry, "Why me? Why now?"

Since Jesus knew about suffering, why shouldn't we? Jesus said: "I have drunk out of that bitter cup which the Father hath given me . . . in taking upon me the sins of the world, in the which I have suffered the will of the Father in all things from the beginning. . . . Thrust your hands into my side, and also that ye may feel the prints of the nails in my hands and in my feet, that ye may know that I am the God of Israel . . . and have been slain for the sins of the world." (3 Nephi 11:11, 14.)

Joseph Smith knew about suffering. He said, "And though I was hated and persecuted for saying that I had seen a vision, yet it was true; and while they were persecuting me, reviling me, and speaking all manner of evil against me falsely for so saying, I was led to say in my heart: Why persecute me for telling the truth?" (Joseph Smith—History: 1:25.)

He might have asked when he prayed, "Why me?" After all, in his first prayer, all he had planned on was a simple answer as to which church he should join.

Moroni, the last Nephite after the destruction of the Nephite civilization and its people, wrote, "I, Moroni, will not deny the Christ: wherefore, I wander withersoever I can for the safety of mine own life" (Moroni 1:3).

Moroni and his father, Mormon, who suffered untold agonies, might well have cried out, "Why me?"

Understanding provides an answer to that question: we are here to be tried. We voted to come down and to be proven to see if God can trust us. Second, we agreed to help the Lord in his work. All the trials we go through shall give us experience. Experience strengthens understanding and develops skills. Experience increases compassion. Experience makes us effective as we help the Lord in his mission.

Even if everyone is to be tried, even if many you know or love are struggling at this moment under adversity of some kind, when it is your problem, your pain, it still hurts. We may not always be noble and strong. Most of us are fainthearted at some point during adversity. For a moment our strength may be small and we, too, might question, "Why me? Why now? Why so much, so much?"

But an echo of the suffering Christ can fill us, if we will listen: "My God, my God, why hast thou forsaken me?" (Mark 15:34).

Or the echo of Joseph Smith, a prisoner in the infamous Liberty Jail, "O God, where art thou? . . . How long shall thy hand be stayed?" (D&C 121:1–2.)

To the true believer, there is promise that can bring comfort at the moment of questioning, "Why me?" "Why now?" "Where art thou?"

Read again 1 Peter 4:12–13 which says: "Beloved, think it not strange concerning the fiery trial which is to try you, as though some strange thing happened unto you: But rejoice, inasmuch as ye are partakers of Christ's sufferings; that, when his glory shall be revealed, ye may be glad also with exceeding joy."

As bad as it can get, there is the assurance that there is purpose, that trials come to all God's followers for their benefit, and that weeping endures only for a night for "joy cometh in the morning" (Psalms 30:5).

The joy will often come not only because the trial is over but also because we know that with God's help we have passed the test. If joy were dependent on the end of trials, we would often be disappointed, for the parade of problems continues; when one trial is done there is another around the proverbial corner.

There are terrible troubles among the Saints. Bizarre things are happening. Hearts are being broken. Testimonies are being tried. Dreams are being dashed. Pressures of all kinds and temptations that were never imagined are all directed at God's choice children. But in D&C 106:5 we learn a critical key: "Therefore, gird up your loins, that you may be the children of light."

When you wonder if the sun will ever shine on you again, spread some shine of your own light and you too will feel the warmth.

For example, following a morning session of general conference several years ago, my phone rang. As I answered, I heard these shocking words: "I have called to say good-bye; I'm committing suicide." An outburst of sobbing followed that cry. I waited. Then gently I spoke calming phrases. As the caller gained some control and repeated the threat with firm conviction of purpose, I was frightened. I knew and loved this woman and I had invested hours in her life. Her heartbreak was real and understandable. But suicide?

It seemed the only answer to her. She explained that the conference had pointed up to her how hopeless her situation was. She had no place in a church where perfection was expected. She had no family any longer. Her marriage sealing was broken, her children had been taken by their father. She had lost the companionship of the Holy Ghost. What purpose was there for her in life? Death could put an end to suffering.

That, of course, is where she was as wrong as she could be. She had forgotten the plan and the law of the harvest. But I let her talk and at last managed to get her to really listen when I suggested a purpose for her life. It was a small beginning, but it was something she suddenly grasped at.

She had been excommunicated. After years of agony she had been rebaptized, although her temple ordinances had not yet been restored. She could understand what other sinners had to go through. There were people out there who were hurting and would welcome an understanding friend. We talked about specific cases and how to put her in touch with people who were ready to move forward. Suicide wasn't an answer for her. She was needed to help others.

She was heartened. And, in fact, the good that she finally did can't be measured. She sought the help of the Lord. Her new project took her mind off herself. She became aware that there was something that she could do that a member in good standing might not be able to do as effectively.

Some years ago I met a certain European man—now deceased—whose body was deformed and bent, from the incredible tortures he suffered as a prisoner during World War II. He let me examine his fingernails that had been mutilated by piercing, uprooting, or pounding during that ordeal. And there were other unspeakable tortures. I have wept as he testified that such dreadful experience was worth it, for it was in that prison camp that he was introduced to the gospel by a member of The Church of Jesus Christ of Latter-day Saints. This brother said that as he came to know Heavenly Father and Jesus he had new purpose for surviving. He prayed for help and strength to endure. He said that the answers to his prayers came in a flood of power from God. God's miracles allowed his survival and ultimate release.

This refiner's fire prepared him to be a great leader in the Church. He taught the truth to his own family and to others. Many were baptized. Many serve in the Church today because of his stalwart example.

President Ezra Taft Benson in a message to today's Saints has expressed alarm as men's hearts fail them spiritually when they are under duress. "Many are giving up heart for the battle of life. . . . As the showdown between good and evil approaches with its accompanying trials and tribulations, Satan is increasingly striving to overcome the Saints with despair, discouragement, despondency, and depression.

"Yet, of all people, we as Latter-day Saints should be the most optimistic and the least pessimistic. For while we know that 'peace shall be taken from the earth, and the devil shall have power over his own dominion,' we are also assured that 'the Lord shall have power over his saints, and shall reign in their midst.' (D&C 1:35–36.)

"With the assurance that the Church shall remain intact with God directing it through the troubled times ahead, it then becomes our individual responsibility to see that each of us remains faithful to the Church and its teachings. 'He that remaineth steadfast and is not overcome, the same shall be saved.' (JS-M 1:11.)" ("Do Not Despair," *Ensign,* Oct. 1986, p. 2.)

Life is school. Of all the trials and tests in life, the critical, overriding challenge is to not "flunk school." Every test, when met by applying gospel principles to the situation, counts toward "graduation."

A person who understands that life is schooling is more likely to benefit from adversity than one who expects only happiness in life—not understanding that life, by the design of our Heavenly Father and the Lord Jesus Christ, can prepare us for a level of even higher learning and understanding.

This awareness of the purpose of life and the plan of salvation may be the place that we start as we try to help someone who is giving in to despair, whose passions under trial have taken over past reason or God's comfort. We cannot bring back the dead, restore the lost, silence enemies, or even eliminate a severe problem plaguing a loved one. But as a willing—and prepared!—agent of the Lord, we can gently introduce the truth about the purpose of life and the principles that govern our growth on our journey here. According to Alma 12:24, "This life became . . . a time to prepare to meet God; a time to prepare for that endless state."

Read again the account of Alma's mission to the Zoramites, found in Alma 31–36. Through him the humble and suffering people were taught to grow in faith in the word of God, which gives the answers to life's problems and the secret to spiritual growth.

Wanting help from God, instead of any other source, is at last the true solution. We start with a seed, a small faith, and follow the careful nurturing steps that bring about the Lord's purposes, the Lord's comfort, and our growth. Alma spoke of the blessing that comes from being compelled into humility because of life's circumstances. When we are humble, we are then ready to learn wisdom, to hear—really hear—the word of God. This learning through experience enhances our efforts to assist others.

When we are pushed, stung, defeated, embarrassed, hurt, rejected, tormented, forgotten—when we are in agony of spirit crying out "why me?" we are in a position to learn something. Inner resources can be stirred under such stress. Hidden strengths awaken that can be a blessing to others.

And we can become closer to God!

If we had everything
that we wanted and needed
without asking
of Heavenly Father,
we would lose sight
of the hand of God
in our lives.

5

Adversity
Brings Us
Closer to God

Adversity can bring us closer to God. When we are in deep need, prayers usually are more fervent and frequent than when we are not.

"Let not your heart be troubled: ye believe in God," said Jesus to his Apostles shortly before he picked up the cross to walk to his crucifixion. Then he prayed for them—out loud—so that they could hear him. "This is life eternal, that they might know thee the only true God, and Jesus Christ, whom thou has sent." (John 14:1; 17:3.)

These promises from God can comfort and sustain us through any kind of demand upon our soul. When we turn to God in prayer—with a needful spirit and a contrite heart and a desire to learn, we will feel the Spirit, the healing.

Sometimes praying is difficult because we haven't developed a close relationship with God. Praying without a relationship with our Father is like trying to have an intimate heart-to-heart talk about your fondest dreams with the ticket-taker at the football game.

With God, it is different, of course. He knows us! He is waiting to be gracious to us, but he does not force his way into our lives. He waits upon us—until our growth and choices make us ready for him.

One of the things we seem to need most in life is a friend who is with us always, upon whom we can count, who loves us unconditionally, and who would never turn against us; a friend whose guidance is based on wisdom and truth. Oh, what a friend to have!

Jesus is such a friend. As we study his life and his teachings, we come to know him. Then we gain confidence before him, and we quickly and surely feel his unfailing love for us.

He wants us to draw close to him so that he can draw close to us. Tribulation is good for us in the sense that it can bring us to our knees as we seek his comfort and guidance; it draws us close to him.

I once asked a group of missionaries what they had learned in the mission field that would help them during the rest of their lives. Many answers came. All of them were supportive of the great learning that the missionary experience brings. But there was one answer that taught me something valuable.

"I have learned something about prayer," one young elder said. "I know that I should *prepare to pray* and then stay on my knees until I feel different! You know, it is like tracting—if I were to go out tracting without my shoes on, I wouldn't last very long. If I seek the Lord without being fully ready, prayer doesn't work either."

Preparing ourselves and then actually praying is a blessed possibility when we are in the midst of affliction.

Involved in a hopeless conflict with a dread enemy, the Nephites begged Mormon to lead them one more time into the war. Mormon's response was sorrowful: "I was without hope, for I knew the judgments of the Lord which should come upon them; for they repented not of their iniquities, but did struggle for their lives without calling upon that Being who created them" (Mormon 5:1).

Aren't we often like these Nephites? We turn to our neighbor, we confess on the golf course to a buddy, we cry to the bishop, we anxiously read the advice column or make an appointment with a counselor. Any or all of these steps may be helpful in some way, but surely calling upon God who created us should be our first and primary response.

The murderer-king in Shakespeare's Hamlet had a problem, too! During his mental anguish he uttered these telling, dramatic words: "Bow, stubborn knees; and, heart with strings of steel, Be soft as sinews of the new-born babe."

Ah, there is an image—a new-born babe—to help us when we struggle to go before God with our heartaches.

It takes time to learn these things, of course, but the sooner we begin the sooner we become.

I recall standing in a hallway with Sister Camilla Kimball, who was waiting for President Spencer W. Kimball to be free of well-wishers. I had noticed a young couple a short distance away who were staring at Sister Camilla. The couple spoke to each other heatedly for a few moments and then suddenly the young wife, heavy with child, positioned herself squarely in front of Sister Kimball and said, "Sister Kimball, my husband says I ought to be exactly like you." Tears took over.

"My dear," comforted Sister Kimball, "O, my dear!"

Then in her practical and self-effacing way, Sister Kimball added, "I wasn't like this at your age, either."

I love that hopeful comment.

I am certain that praying for endurance, for self-improvement, or for strength and guidance to reach special goals requires perspective.

A friend of mine was going into a second marriage and someone told her the story about another woman in the same situation who turned to her son and asked him, "Son, will you give me away at my wedding?"

"Give you away?" the son exclaimed. "I can't give you away, I haven't finished with you yet!"

Like this son with his mother, God isn't finished with us yet. With our hand in his we will grow.

Consider King Benjamin's counsel to his people: "Believe in God; believe that he is, and that . . . he has all wisdom, and all power, both in heaven and in earth; believe that man doth not comprehend all the things which the Lord can comprehend" (Mosiah 4:9).

We need to understand that God understands things we don't understand yet. We need to remember that he is the creator of *all* things, including us and the plan of our testing, growth, and reward.

During Alma's ministry he visited an area where people discriminated against their own brothers and sisters simply because these brothers and sisters were poverty-stricken. So far away from gospel living had the affluent ones drifted that they had lost all love for those less fortunate than they. Alma had little missionary success with these wealthy discriminators. Some of the poor strugglers, however, came to him for help. These people were "esteemed by their brethren as dross; therefore they were poor as to the things of the world; and also they were poor in heart" (Alma 32:3).

When Alma heard their story, he turned with joy toward the spokesman for the group. He explained to these people that *because* of their afflictions they were blessed—they were made humble and now they were *prepared* to hear the word of God.

Alma said, "It is well that ye are cast out of your synagogues, that ye may be humble, and that ye may learn wisdom" (Alma 32:12). He taught them that because they were humble and had turned to God they would be blessed. Then he went on to teach the mighty lesson we should all learn. He explained that being humble prepares us to learn. *But how much better off we are, if we seek God's will, word, and way without being forced into humility.* As Alma says, we will be "more blessed" (v. 14).

There are many blessings as well as purposes in prayer. Drawing close to God is a way of witnessing his hand in our lives. Even if our requests aren't answered exactly as we had hoped they might be, we eventually feel the Spirit of the Lord with us even in our disappointment.

Prayer is often the avenue through which we receive the promptings of the Spirit in our affairs: we can be comforted or our conscience can be pricked, and we'll feel restless and uneasy. The following story of Lee and Sandi illustrates this.

Lee's problem wasn't one of those nice clean trials, such as financial disaster or terminal cancer. People finally get over things like that—one way or another.

Lee's on-going problem was his marriage. The relationship was anything but satisfying, and it was the cause of stressful suffering and deep unhappiness.

Backgrounds of the marriage partners can sometimes create problems. Lee had gone to Brigham Young University on an athletic scholarship. He wasn't a Latter-day Saint. In fact, his life had been geared to something quite different from the sheltered discipline of Mormon values and standards. But once at BYU, Lee had "gone with the flow." When in Happy Valley, do as the citizens you like do. So he did. And being basically a good and sensitive person, Lee liked the new way he was living. He didn't really understand the details of the gospel, but when the challenge to become baptized was given, Lee accepted. He could go to church with his friends.

After a time, Lee's friends began marrying in the temple, so he wanted to marry in the temple. And he did; it was the thing to do.

His bride, Sandi, was a girl with a background as far removed from Lee's as her home state was from his home state. She came from a five-generation Mormon family who had always lived in the same little Mormon town. They were stalwarts and leaders in the stake.

Lee came from a glittering metropolis with all the accompanying temptations. His family was broken and scattered. He was on his own to do what he wanted. He had ideals and goals but no guidance.

Sandi was grateful to have a chance to be married in the temple—a lot of girls didn't make it. Sandi had her temple marriage. Lee had his bride. He now fit in perfectly with the rest of his former roommates.

Opposites may attract in some cases, but the bloom was soon off that "appropriate" marriage. It wasn't what either of them had expected.

Sandi wanted a man who would be first to volunteer for the welfare farm assignments or temple sealing sessions and who would stand at the ward pulpit on Sundays in a position of authority. She wanted a man exactly like her father—a public figure, an example. Sandi prayed that Lee would change.

Lee, on the other hand, hadn't had a father like Sandi's. What Lee wanted was what he had *not* had in his own early years. He wanted warmth and gentle caring, all the love and companionship and stable serenity that he had hungered for always. He didn't know much about rules and regulations governing Mormon families or what temples and welfare farms had to do with marriage, but he was interested in being a good husband, father, and provider. He used careful planning for the family's future. And he loved his children and wanted them to love and appreciate him for what he *was* good at.

Sandi seemed an ideal LDS mother. Her house wasn't always immaculate but she loved her children and devoted herself to church work. It was her whole life. And everybody including Lee knew it. Lee, however, thought he should come before some "extra" church activity and be at least on an equal basis with the children. It hurt him deeply when the choices went against him.

As the relationship soured, Lee suffered because he was without a secure support system and because he did not have a deep understanding of the gospel. He fell into despair. Like a cripple who at last accepts that he will never walk again, Lee finally realized that happiness for him wouldn't come with this woman.

Sandi fell out of love with Lee because he didn't meet her particular vision of the ideal LDS man. He didn't do anything wrong; he just wasn't as anxiously engaged as she wanted him to be—and she continually reminded him of it.

Their solution had been to put up a good front in public but to shut each other out in private. They lived lives of quiet desperation. As the children grew into awareness of the conflict, the situation darkened.

One day Lee became aware that his anguish and sleepless nights had taken an ugly turn. He felt that the only way out was divorce or suicide. The only thing that saved him, for a time, was his high emotional and financial investment in his family. He couldn't afford divorce, yet he was hurting and frightened. There just had to be another alternative.

Lee began to pray just to hang on. Even endurance is a form of growth.

As for Sandi, one day she and I were discussing their situation. With resounding tones Sandi said to me, "My sole purpose in life is to see to it that my children get to the celestial kingdom." Virtue was shining about her.

I ignored this holier-than-thou demeanor for the moment and questioned, "Don't you want a partner for all eternity?

Don't you want to be in the celestial kingdom with your family?''

Sandi was shocked at the question. Until that moment, she had blamed all of their troubles on Lee, forgetting that he supported the family very comfortably, forgetting that he worked with honor as a professional at Church headquarters, forgetting that he was a loyal family man and regular church goer—even attending tithing settlement. Forgetting these things, Sandi complained that Lee simply wasn't the same kind of Mormon that her father was. He hadn't grown. How could he get into the celestial kingdom?

Her view, of course, was narrow.

To try to help her, I ventured that no amount of success with one's children—who also have their free agency—can make up for failure with temple covenants. Celestial kingdoms were about marriage! Surely she had some responsibility to help her husband make it to that glorious place which she herself seemed so confident of reaching. How could she fail; she had a host of Church jobs.

Laughingly I reminded Sandi of Camelot when Guinevere had been listening to Lancelot brag about his virtues and then asked him, "Have you jousted with humility lately?"

Humility is a virtue, too.

Then in a more serious tone, I urged Sandi not only to read but to ponder D&C 25, paying particular attention to verses 5 and 14. This is the Lord's counsel to Emma regarding her relationship and duties to Joseph: she was to be a "comfort unto . . . thy husband, in his afflictions, with consoling words, in the spirit of meekness. . . . Let thy soul delight in thy husband.''

The section ends with the statement, "And verily, verily, I say unto you, that this is my voice unto all" (v. 16). Even unto Sandi.

Love is the first law of the gospel, as is learning to abide basic laws. Sandi and Lee needed to look to their loving and their learning. They needed to cultivate understanding patience with each other.

The story of Lee and Sandi is the story of all married couples, in a way. Even people born in the same home town with similar backgrounds are different, aren't they? They, too, have to overcome and accommodate. They must seek God's direction and an understanding of his principles so that his will can be done for their family.

At this writing, the family of Lee and Sandi still stands. For the sake of the children it stands. Because of prayers for endurance, it stands. But they must yet learn real love.

Walking a rough path of enduring is one way. The higher principle is to pray for growth and understanding, direction and proper action—while one is enduring! Drawing closer to God in times of trouble means listening to his will.

The matter of listening to God when we do seek him in prayer can be valued better if we consider the counsel that Alma gave to his son Helaman. It is good counsel for us, too. "I beseech of thee that thou wilt hear my words . . . ; for I do know that whosoever shall put their trust in God shall be supported in their trials, and their troubles, and their afflictions, and shall be lifted up at the last day" (Alma 36:3).

If we refuse to listen to God, our prayers are empty. Fulfillment cannot come. That is the condition of prayer.

Because we don't always know what is in store for us, cultivating proper prayer, drawing close to God even when circumstances of life aren't particularly demanding, can prepare us for inevitable problems along life's path. We are already in touch with God.

Our family knelt around the master bed during a period when all of the children were home. There were eight of us then whose lives were inextricably intertwined by birth, choice, and temple sealing. We had just moved from our crowded little house to a larger but shabbier place. Our work was cut out for us, but our budget was tight. We had discussed these realities of our lives one more time just before we knelt to pray.

We wanted this move and the risks involved to be right for us, of course.

We wanted all things pertaining to this change in our lives to be according to God's will for our family.

We wanted his watch over our investment.

We wanted the Holy Spirit to dwell there and permeate our lives.

We wanted protection and peace.

But we also wanted our house to be handsome one day. The basic structure of the big, old house was fine. However, it needed a tremendous amount of work to make it an environment in which we felt we could flourish. While we weren't out to impress anybody with what we had, each child and adult had definite dreams about what the house should ultimately be like.

We also wanted to be able to afford the renovations and redecorating. Does all this sound familiar?

Naturally we had some large challenges, not the least of which were to keep our value system up front, to keep contention low, and to stifle foolishness, falseness, selfishness, fatigue, and delusions of grandeur.

We needed to pray. Besides, churches and temples were dedicated to God, so why not our home? Kneeling around the master bed, then, we dedicated our home.

My husband was head of our home in a very real and vital way. He asked each of us to take a turn in these little dedicatory services. I prayed first. Then in the order of their birth, each of the children prayed, expressing their feelings and commitment about the new home. Then my husband gave the dedicatory prayer.

It was wonderful. We were of one heart and one mind. The sweet spirit of the Lord filled every soul. And it was amazing to us that in prayer the details of our various expectations became clear to all.

Time passed. This house was never really "finished." There was never time enough nor money enough to refurbish it in the manner we had dreamed of when we moved in and prayed our dreams before God. In fact, our finances got worse instead of better. There were other demanding, diverse trials during these years.

But that day of dedication helped us immeasurably. Through our struggles along the way, we kept referring to the dedicatory prayer when dreams were fresh and spirits humble. We were in these circumstances together from the start, with God, and we pulled together.

That house became our corner of heaven on earth. It was not a show place, after all. This was the period when missions, weddings, and grandchildren happened. We felt so close to heaven there because we needed God's help often—not to decorate a house but to solve life's problems with eternal reach, according to his will.

The importance of praying in anticipation of inevitable testings in life was part of our dedication ceremony. It is part of the message of this book, too.

Some time ago I was wheeled back into a hospital room following surgical procedures that required that I lay absolutely quiet and unmoving for eight hours. My surgeon roused me from the effects of the anesthetic and took my hand while he spoke distinctly and emphatically to be certain that I heard and understood. He told me that I must not move—no matter what—for the specified period of hours. He sternly said that my life depended upon it.

Again he asked, "Do you understand, Elaine? Your life depends upon it!"

"Easy!" I mused. Understand? Why I welcomed such bliss. I had come into that hospital one tired lady. Eight hours of uninterrupted rest was welcome. I'd have no trouble not moving.

As soon as nurses, family, and doctor left the room, I was wide awake. Naturally, with the chance to sleep on and on, my mind wouldn't cooperate. I counted flaws in the ceiling as well as lambs in some make-believe field. Soon I ached for a more comfortable position. Later I decided that just a very slight shift in position couldn't make any difference—nobody would know . . .

Fortunately, a get-away-with-it-if-you-can attitude is a rationale that won't work when the echo of "your life depends upon it" comes to mind.

So I gritted my teeth and endured, not moving. Soon my jaws ached along with the rest of my body as I lay in a flat-back position with sandbags along each side to keep me in place.

It was tough. And because what I did mattered, I prayed for help. As the hours dragged on, my own will weakened. My prayers became anxious pleas. After a time a flash of understanding came to me. Enduring—simply enduring under stress was unrewarding. I decided that the time would pass more pleasantly and profitably if I directed my thoughts. So I remembered joyful times; I counted blessings. Then I drew close to the Lord and talked some things over with him that were important to all the rest of my life.

My attitude of mere grit changed to one of willing submission geared to constructive learning. That change in attitude made all the difference in how I passed the time.

Life is like that. When we can't change a circumstance, we can either grit our teeth and hang on with clenched jaws, or we can submit cheerfully until change occurs. And with God's help we can learn some important lessons. We can feel peace.

As we look at the various kinds of trouble and stress, the trials and heartbreak that people today are tested with, some problems seem more serious and harder to take than others. But God has promised us that we will not be tested beyond what we can endure—even if we bring trouble to ourselves— because he can help us climb back out. He helps us with his principles and he helps us with his encompassing Spirit and he helps us through his agents.

It seems to me that the most important knowledge available to mortals is that we are children of a living God, that Jesus is our Elder Brother, our Redeemer. He cares about us and has all power to help us in the ways most important for us.

Overwhelmingly, people testify of this. When they have suffered and turned to Heavenly Father in a sweet hour of prayer, they do witness his caring. I know that this is true.

The price we pay to become acquainted with God and his will and his ways inevitably proves to be a price well worth it.

Consider these beautiful words written by President Ezra Taft Benson:

> It is a great blessing . . . to have an inner peace, to have an assurance, to have a spirit of serenity, an inward calm during times of strife and struggle, during times of sorrow and reverses. It is soul-satisfying to know that God is at the helm, that he is mindful of his children, and that we can with full confidence place our trust in him. I believe that all the truly great men of the earth have been men who trusted in God and who have striven to do that which is right as they understood the right. (*Improvement Era*, June 1954, p. 406.)

One of these truly great men was my husband's grandfather, George Q. Cannon. He was a member of the First Presidency of the Church under Brigham Young, John Taylor, and Wilford Woodruff. He was speaking about the 98th section of the Doctrine and Covenants, verses 1 through 3, when he said, "Though your prayers may not be answered immediately, if they are offered in the name of Jesus and in faith, nothing being left undone by you that is required, they will *live* on the records of Heaven and in the remembrance of the Lord and yet bear fruit" (*Millennial Star,* Vol. 25, pp. 74).

However and whenever peace may come, it does come. It comes according to God's wisdom. It may come with a sweeping feeling within us. It may come through another person's help or counsel. It may come through scripture study when a passage stands forth with unusual clarity. But it comes because of our closeness to God and because of his goodness to us.

Spiritual maturity is
understanding that
we cannot blame
anybody else
for our problems.

6

Adversity—
What's in It for Me?

Adversity—what's in it for me? Well, consider the remarkable accounts of prisoners in concentration camps. Of what worth was such a trial?

Life was dreadful in those infamous places of suffering, abuse, humiliation, and hopelessness. It was the Nazi era of World War II and man's inhumanity to man seemed at its worst. Fear and despair were the constant companions particularly of those in the "death section." For one group, things changed somewhat when Corrie ten Boom, an unusual Dutch lady, came into their midst—Corrie and her little Bible! She had miraculously smuggled her Bible into the barracks, past guards so searching that total nudity had to be endured. But she managed to keep the Bible, and adversity was turned into a blessing.

Death camps were well named, but as Corrie began reading God's word to the ever-growing circle of listeners, hope came with learning. Life after certain death—and all that means—became a comforting promise. It would be all right, whatever happened now.

Their schoolroom was a pitiful, crowded, uncomfortable, cold, sparse, dim barrack. The subject was survival, at least of the soul! In adversity they were ready to learn.

In her book, *The Hiding Place,* Corrie wrote about the secret and simple services that were held each possible evening for Bible reading:

> A small light bulb cast a wan yellow circle on the wall, and here an ever larger group of women gathered.
>
> They were services like no others, these times in Barracks 28. A single meeting night might include a recital of the Magnificat in Latin by a group of Roman Catholics, a whispered hymn by some Lutherans, and a sotto-voce chant by Eastern Orthodox women. With each moment the crowd around us would swell, packing the nearby platforms, hanging over the edges, until the high structures groaned and swayed.
>
> At last either Betsie or I would open the Bible. Because only the Hollanders could understand the Dutch text we would translate aloud in German. And then we would hear the life-giving words passed back along the aisles in French, Polish, Russian, Czech, back into Dutch. They were little previews of heaven, these evenings beneath the light bulb. I would think of Haarlem, each substantial church set behind its wrought-iron fence and its barrier of doctrine. And I would know again that in darkness God's truth shines most clear. (Corrie ten Boom, *The Hiding Place* [New York: Bantam Books, 1971], p. 201.)

Viktor Frankl learned many important lessons and has shared them over the years following his own period of trial in concentration camps. Though he was a Jewish prisoner, restrained without cause, he came to realize that even in the worst of times, life has vital meaning if we will but look for it. He learned that "everything can be taken from a man but one thing; the last of the human freedoms—to choose one's attitude in any given set of circumstances, to choose one's own way." (Viktor E. Frankl, *Man's Search for Meaning* [New York: Simon and Schuster, Touchstone Books, 1962], p. 65.)

An amazing peace can come, even a lift to the spirit, when we put our minds in the mood of selective learning. Complaining about a problem only rehearses the pain. But sorting out the elements of the trial can reveal valuable truth.

Resourcefulness and unflagging faith—finally achieved—can move people forward in times of trial. There's another reason why we may need adversity in our lives. For example, Connie moved with her family to a Third World country when her father's business assigned him there.

She was fifteen, and the adjustment was difficult. School was the worst. Of course, she missed her friends at home, but that wasn't the real problem. The youth in this land strange to her thought she was strange. They mimicked her accent. Her lunch hours were lonely, and she became the target for jeers— "Yankee go home!" And she wanted to. She was hurt and angry—even resentful toward her father. Making friends and having fun was so much of what life was supposed to be about at this age, and it wasn't happening there.

When I visited that country, Connie and I talked about turning a negative into a positive. I told her about my years in the fabric business with bolts of colorfast fabric all around— except the Indian madras, a cotton fabric of inimitable quality that was not colorfast. At first people wouldn't buy it. Then we hit on an idea for sales. The fact that colors were *guaranteed* to fade and run when the fabric was laundered was promoted as part of the fabric's appeal. It was a sensational success. People looked at madras in a new light and bought it.

Connie caught the message. Instead of trying to blend in with the natives, unsuccessfully, Connie appeared on campus as the all-American girl in western togs. She was deliberately different. She carried American magazines for youth (including the *New Era*) and willingly shared them. She shared her cassettes of American music. She laughed at herself along with them. The other students became fascinated. And then the family began serving typical American food to Connie's new friends so they could see how these "foreigners" ate. Banana splits, hamburgers, and chocolate chip cookies were favorites.

In another instance, a young career woman, whom we will call Jane, moved to a small Utah college town after a brilliant beginning in a big city. Her credentials were excellent: a college education, a mission, corporate experience with an executive-level income, enhancing adventures with theater, dining, opera, and travel. She'd had it all—almost. She hadn't had what she really wanted—a husband, a home, and children.

The years passed, and she found herself with a new job at the local university, living in a house in a neighborhood of struggling families. She was a chic dresser among women

locked into maternity clothes or grubbies. The serene decor
and orderliness of her home were a sharp contrast to the
others' two-bedroom places crammed with children, cribs,
and a year's supply of confusion.

She was different. At best, neighbors were certain that with
so little in common there could be no real relating. She might
even be a threat. She could stir restlessness.

Single and successful in that familial environment spelled
deep loneliness for Jane. The ward setting wasn't a big im-
provement. She had looked forward to being in a standard
ward after years of being with singles. But here the topics for
sermons and class discussions seemed to program her out.
They were strictly family oriented.

Bitterness began creeping in. Where was her "Mr. Right,"
with whom an exchange of cherishing could happen? Where
was personal worth in a society based on the number of babies
a woman had? Where was fulfillment of her patriarchal blessing about celestial life? And, practically speaking, what was a
single girl with heart and dreams and needs and goals supposed to do in a place like this after working hours?

She could have cried a lot, pacified herself with fattening
treats, excused away self-indulgence at the local cinema, or
hidden away with a romance novel and become increasingly
neurotic. But she hadn't—yet. Then one Sunday she let self-
pity take over.

The morning dragged painfully. Loneliness closed in upon
her, and by the time her ward's meetings were supposed to
start she had come to a decision. She wasn't going back. Never
again would she sit in church all alone on the back bench
watching all those families marching in wearing parenting like
a red windsock wafting overhead.

What good was there in going to church? She felt worse
when she went than when she stayed home. For weeks she'd
fought resentment. She'd managed to stifle the urge to stand
up in church and tell those people the awful truth about themselves and their narrow, excluding vision.

She'd tried to make friends. They didn't have time for her.
She didn't fit in. They had nothing in common—she couldn't
talk endlessly about labor pains.

This Sunday this rehash of hurt brought tears and Jane gave in to sobs, throwing herself on the bed in utter despair and self-pity.

At last, spent emotionally, she rose and went into the kitchen to get a little something to eat. As she responded to childhood training to ask Heavenly Father to bless the food for which she was grateful, Jane was flooded with her need for God's help. She dropped to her knees by her glass-topped table and poured out her heart.

Oh, she had always prayed regularly, but this time was different. This time her heart was broken, her spirit contrite. But most of all, her decision to give up the Church frightened her. She needed God's help.

Her prayer was swift and direct. "Heavenly Father show me the way. There is no other help but thee. Please, Father, show me the way!"

Now a series of things happened. A knock at her door stirred her from her prayer. One of the little children on the block needed a ride to church. She was late. Daddy was out of town, Mommy was ill, the neighbors had already gone. Could Jane help? Jane could!

At church the topic of a sermon was the story of the prodigal son. Jane knew the story well, but this time, as the speaker applied the parable to life now, her heart began to pound.

"The prodigal arose and came to his father," explained the speaker. "[And] when he was yet a great way off, his father saw him, and had compassion, and ran, and fell on his neck, and kissed him" (Luke 15:20).

It wasn't a pat on the shoulder; it was a feast and a showering of gifts; it was a mighty rising to the occasion. Would God do less for his children?

Jane vowed a vow. She'd solve her problem with Heavenly Father's help. She'd get herself ready to go to the temple for her endowments. (In the temple, differences aren't as marked as they are in neighborhoods.) She'd study the scriptures for support and direction. She'd really converse with the Father in prayer rather than merely reciting familiar phrases. Instead of leaving the Church, she'd return to the fold in spirit as well as in body.

Her fervent prayer before church that Sunday and the swift events following it served her spirit well. There was help and there was hope.

Jane hasn't married yet, but she has found peace and a place in her neighborhood.

There is an exchange of learning and teaching each other along the way. She helps with home decoration and household organization. They help her with food storage. As a guest at family home evenings, she is learning another side of the gospel as well as the miracle of growth in life from infancy.

Now she has regular "Pasta Parties" at her home for neighbors—married and single. They're informal affairs with the guest list thoughtfully structured to encourage a comfortable mix and good conversation, and even to proselyte a non-member friend from campus.

She is the best birthday party giver for the eight-year-olds the block has ever had. And she is "our friend Jane" to tired parents and starry-eyed children alike. She's joined in ward camp and ski trips. Jane is far from lonely any longer.

The bread of charity cast upon a soul or a neighborhood comes back a hundredfold into a lonely heart.

Lonely people in any situation can go on being lonely and miserable, or, if they are humble and contrite enough during adversity to really listen to what God is saying, they can grow in strength, comfort, and usefulness.

In Doctrine and Covenants 18:19, we learn that if we do not have faith, hope, and charity we can do nothing. The opposite is, of course, true—with them we can do anything.

Losing hope, being hopeless and helpless, is to deny the power of God. He knows us and our timetable in growth and purpose. Our heartache is his.

Louise lived alone, trapped in a wheelchair. A parade of problems plagued her. She had only one lung and no use of her lower body. Her finances were in a constant state of crisis. Her marriage dissolved, and she had a little girl to rear alone. Her loss of personal beauty startled her and tugged at her self-esteem. Her independent nature and personal pride had to give way, publicly and privately.

Then she began applying gospel principles to her adversity. What could she learn from this trial? Louise went through the paces of spiritual growth, meeting her test. When the time came she was beautifully prepared to meet Heavenly Father, leaving behind her many grateful people to remember her example.

Each morning over the years Louise practiced what she labeled her exercise in joy—a kind of fervent blessing counting session. Upon awakening she would address our Heavenly Father in gratitude for another day. Each day was a bonus, she said. Each day was a chance to learn something more and to hone herself spiritually, to understand the plight of others, whatever it might be. She would commence her exercise in joy at the top of her head, and thank God for hair—some people don't have any on their heads. She had that! She'd move through eyes that could see and a mind that could think, and so on.

Trapped physically, she soared spiritually, well beyond people who hadn't suffered such adversity.

Imagine, an exercise in joy! She didn't curse God and die, though she was akin to Job. She gave thanks and lived— anyway. And she'll walk again in another life.

LaRue Longden, a former counselor in the general presidency of the Young Women, was a ward Young Women president at the time of the serious illness of her little daughter. Babies were hard to come by in that family—this little daughter was the first one, and now she was threatened. Fear clutched at the hearts of Brother and Sister Longden as they knelt in prayer during a crisis of the illness. Then, at that very moment, word came that their little daughter had passed away. It wasn't what they had in mind. Why hadn't their prayers been answered? Why not the miracle?

It happened that after the funeral, in tribute to their beloved ward president, young women and their leaders held flowers and formed an aisle for Sister Longden and her husband to walk past them.

During this time of intense emotion, LaRue became aware that the girls were watching her. "I had to live what I had been teaching," she explained. "I had to be an example of what I really believed before these impressionable girls."

So, she lifted her chin and smiled upon her young women, her eyes swimming in tears for the daughter who wouldn't grow to be their age in this life. Adversity heightened her awareness of the precious gift life is for young women.

A fourteen-year-old girl survived a serious bout with cancer, but she'll never be able to bear children. Being a mother was all she'd dreamed about as she played with her dolls, while other girls ran for the baseball field.

"The Young Women motto helped me," Molly told me. "The Lord is the strength of my life" (Psalm 27:1). The motto became more than words to recite with her class or to embroider on a wall hanging. She lived by it. It helped her meet her test and determine to be a super teacher of children. She could do it, too, with God's help all the way.

Already this young woman is in constant demand as a mother's helper because she brings into the home a special love and skill.

Geneva, a gifted friend, whose illness for years has kept her from walking, would not give up her Relief Society visiting teaching assignment. She owed too much to Heavenly Father —in spite of (or because of!) being denied the miracle of healing. As a visiting teacher she had unique problems because of her physical condition. But she managed. She phoned her ladies ahead of time. After being loaded into her special vehicle, she drove to their homes, honked the horn, and welcomed them into her car. There the message was given, the focus on heaven enjoyed, the example set, and the burdens lifted because of the outpouring of the spirit that such caring creates.

For many years Rich struggled, almost fruitlessly, to make a living. He had a fine wife and five good children who had become breadwinners in a real sense. The family survived because of their industrious ways. They sold produce from the home garden. They carried paper routes, delivered groceries after school, tended children, helped with household chores for families who could afford to pay them for this service.

The more they added to the family income, the more Rich resented the fact that he needed their help, the more certain he was of his failure as a provider and as a father. He could bring children into the world, but he couldn't take care of their worldly needs.

He was thinking about this one day as he sat in his truck on the edge of a lookout point. It was some distance from their little home. The view of the ocean and islands and port activity was spectacular. The Northwest had the loveliest scenery anywhere, Rich admitted darkly, but it didn't have a place for him in its economic system.

Rich had driven to this viewpoint late in the afternoon of a particularly bitter day, fully intending to drive his battered pickup over the high cliff and end this ridiculous existence. The only thing he could say about himself was that he'd been faithful to his wife. It seemed a small comfort.

As his thoughts took him to his wife, he warmed to memories of their early life together. Mostly it had been good, but the struggle had gotten to her, too. His whole being ached in anguish as he thought of how heavy her load was. The shame of his failure as a husband brought the unfamiliar sting of tears to his eyes.

Do grown men cry? Or were tears just another sign of his own weakness? As he wept, Rich reached for the tissue box his wife kept in the truck cab. It was what he'd once described as silly. One of the children had made it for Mom's Christmas. In quick-stitch around the cover were the words, "You are a child of God, too!"

He studied the words. He felt a faint inner stirring. It was meant for him, too!

The plan to drive off the cliff and lose his life so that he didn't have to face it any longer was out of step with a child of God, Rich suddenly realized. But what could he do? Where was help?

He cried out to God. His prayers were urgent, his heart heaving with emotion and awareness and need.

At last, when he drove back home, he felt a certain peace. If his family could take it, he could too. Life wasn't over yet.

But things didn't get better for Rich. They got worse. A few weeks later, his wife was killed in a head-on collision. Rich became the sole parent in the home.

Rich's prayers then were full of need for comfort and understanding and support. But there was deep gratitude there, too. He knew God lived. He knew that he had been stopped from taking his own life by a higher power than his own will. He knew that he could be helped again for the sake of the children.

Interestingly enough, the neighbors and ward members shifted into a new gear. Through Rich's adversity, they grew in some important ways, too. They had judged Rich harshly before. Now sympathy and understanding surfaced, and they were there to help this family over its hurdle.

Rich was given an opportunity for employment with a suitable wage that would allow the children to run the family home as the mother once had, instead of being out of the home long hours to earn wages.

But even more significant to Rich was the return of sweetness in the home. There was a sureness that God loved them—as well as their neighbors—and that he was mindful of them in their adversity. They were more determined to always be people whom God could trust.

What's good about adversity in life? Besides personal growth, it is a time when we can be proven trustworthy before God. One thinks of Job 23:10: "He knoweth the way that I take: when he hath tried me, I shall come forth as gold."

When adversity strikes in any of its forms, seek to learn something from the experience but also look for the blessing, the hidden gift.

Every burden on the back
can be a gift in the hands.

7

Adversity— A Blessing in Disguise

Testing and troubles give us the blessings of experience and of drawing closer to God. Through adversity our character is proven. When considered in this light, every burden has a gift in its hand. When we cope with adversity according to God's laws, ultimately we'll sense the gift.

Perhaps you've seen the bumper sticker that reads, "Am I having any fun yet?" That may be a good question to ask ourselves when we get belted with a difficult test or a crashing disappointment. An even better question we could ask is "What possible blessing is there in this ordeal?" That kind of perspective can help us to cope more effectively and to find the gift, the blessing in adversity.

Countless remarkable Saints have proven that living of gospel principles modifies attitude which, in turn, modifies adversity into blessings. Ordinary people become extraordinary ones.

Some years ago we were having some kitchen remodeling done. The foreman on the job brought a carpenter to meet me. The carpenter folded his arms across his chest and stood there looking me up and down, as he acknowledged the introduction.

"So, you're Elaine Cannon. Well, let me tell you something. My wife has had seventeen children, and she looks better than you do!"

We laughed together, and I knew we were going to get along fine. He was proud of his wife, and he was honest! As the days passed I learned a lot about Joe. His story is a great example of the blessing of adversity.

Joe explained that he had been a partner in a construction company until a few years before. Then his partner had lost control of his life—he withdrew the fifty thousand dollars in the company account, charged heavily on the company cards, and skipped town in a new luxury car. Joe was left with a bad credit rating and no capital with which to run the company. And he couldn't find work because it was a time of severe economic slump.

The oldest two of Joe's seventeen children were in the mission field; the third was ready to go. The family's resources reached the crisis stage, and the spiritual fiber of the family dwindled as well.

They fasted, they prayed, they tried to get their lives more in order. It was hard to be loving and patient with this kind of pressure and failure plaguing the family.

Finally they were forced to accept Church welfare for a time. Joe's pride suffered, but there was no other way.

One day Joe had taken his pickup truck out to the valley west of Salt Lake to Welfare Square to pick up the supplies for his large family. As he drove along the freeway toward his home, helplessness overcame him. He was a man who had worked hard all his life, and to be subjected to the humiliation of depending upon others for his keep seemed more than he could bear.

"It was then that heartbreak hit full force," said Joe, with tears beginning to well in his eyes. "I looked at those hands for a moment, then took them off the wheel and held them toward the sky, shouting to God. 'Look at these hands,' I cried out loud. 'Look at them. God, give me work!' "

Joe was thoughtful before he continued the details of this remarkable experience. Then he said softly, "You know, Sister Cannon, right then I heard a voice inside of my mind, just as you are hearing mine. It said to me, 'Be still, and take it!' And when I had learned humility, patience, and gratitude, I found work. And you know," Joe continued, "soon after I found work I was called to serve in the bishopric. One of the first things I had to do was help one of those formerly privileged rich ones accept welfare when the bottom dropped out of his business."

In this world full of adversity, I am struck by the importance of this story. Joe and his family had prayed and fasted, yet it seemed that heaven was deaf to their need.

When Joe was at last brokenhearted and contrite enough to really cry out his anguish before God (and the condition of the heart not the loudness of the cry determines whether we are ready), he heard the voice. Now, the voice didn't tell him to drive to such and such a street and go in a building with tall columns where a job would be waiting; it said to be still and take it!

His experience was helpful to others. His adversity was a preparation; it was a blessing to more than himself.

Adversity, when we look for the blessing in it, can prepare us to be an effective part of the Lord's work here on earth in bringing to pass the immortality and eternal life of man.

Adversity takes on many guises, and God needs many helpers to do his work each day. We forget self when our compassion is stirred for another who is more needful or who has fewer inner resources or less understanding of life and the plan than we might have. We stretch ourselves in their behalf. We reach, we touch a life, and for both of us, our troubles are modified.

We lose our life in the service that lifts someone else. Then we find it, this life of ours! At last, we may even come to be grateful to God for our troubles—we wouldn't trade ours for the trials of others!

At a luncheon of old school friends a woman whose husband had died suddenly of a heart attack was complaining with her friends about her hardship. "If only he would come down and talk to me for a moment," she sobbed. "There are so many things I don't know anything about. Why doesn't he come to me?"

"Maybe I can help you," another woman said softly. "Since we last saw each other years ago, I have buried two husbands. I know something about grief, confusion, and heartbreak. Let's talk about it after."

Two husbands! That ought to prepare a person for reaching out in compassion as well as wisdom to a newcomer to grief. It also gave her opportunities for graduate school training and years of valuable contribution to the community as she worked in top executive levels. And she reared two fine children besides.

Many times the matter of stewardship comes into my mind as I watch people struggle with trouble. I hear so much of heartbreak and anger and depression that when I watch someone going through the phases of a certain kind of trial I want to whisper encouragement of another kind to them. "Be a good steward of this opportunity. Learn the lesson well! Gather wisdom and skill to share. So many out there need your kind of know-how."

Life is tough. So is becoming useful. So is growing.

C. S. Lewis wrote of the need for people to get a higher vision of themselves and what the Lord has in mind for them. The suggestion is a familiar one to many:

> Imagine yourself as a living house. God comes in to rebuild that house. At first, perhaps, you can understand what He is doing. He is getting the drains right and stopping the leaks in the roof and so on: you knew that those jobs needed doing and so you are not surprised. But presently He starts knocking the house about in a way that hurts abominably and does not seem to make sense. What on earth is He up to? The explanation is that He is building quite a different house from the one you thought of—throwing out a new wing here, putting on an extra floor there, running up towers, making courtyards. You thought you were going to be made into a decent little cottage: but He is building a palace. (*Mere Christianity* [New York: Macmillan Publishing Co., Inc., Macmillan Paperbacks Edition, 1960], p. 174.)

Life is learning obedience.

Even Jesus learned obedience by suffering. We can learn obedience.

We can learn compassion.

We can learn to think and plan and ponder the paths of our feet, as suggested in Proverbs 4:26.

We can learn the goodness of people and their willingness to sacrifice for us.

We can learn that gospel principles suffice.

We can gain a vision of the purpose of life and the magnificence of its opportunities.

We can have our appetite whetted for the promise of glories now beyond our understanding.

We can learn that God lives and loves us anyway.

There are countless examples of people who lived in other times in other places whose trials and tribulations have proven them as trusted servants and witnesses of God. And they have been a blessing to their peers.

Daniel as one of the choice sons of Israel was taken captive by an enemy nation to be raised up for a wicked king's own purposes. The best of the lot of captives were to be fed from the king's own table. This was supposed to be a favor but for Daniel this meant trouble. Wine and meat were against his standards as a man of God. Though his life was at risk he reasoned with the guard to serve him grains for a period of time. At last the guard agreed. Daniel withstood the test and was blessed with physical well-being and hidden treasures of knowledge. He found favor with the king, and thus was able to serve his people.

Enoch, slow of speech and lacking confidence, was greatly tried when he was called to serve the Lord in a public way. He worried, "I . . . am but a lad, and all the people hate me; for I am slow of speech; wherefore am I thy servant?" (Moses 6:31).

His was a test of obedience, and whether he liked the test or not, Enoch showed through his willingness to respond to the call that he could be trusted. And one day "as Enoch spake forth the words of God, the people trembled, and could not stand in his presence" (Moses 6:47). He was blessed for meeting his test in ways he could not have dreamed of at first. We can draw strength from his strength. Our faith can deepen by remembering his sturdy faith.

Father Lehi explained to his son Jacob about the importance of keeping faithful under affliction and being trustworthy in spite of persecution. He said, "Jacob, . . . *thou knowest the greatness of God; and he shall consecrate thine afflictions for thy gain.* Wherefore, thy soul shall be blessed, and thou shalt dwell safely. . . . For it must needs be, that there is an opposition in all things." (2 Nephi 2:2–3, 11; italics added.)

Job's struggles are well-known. His story has become state-of-the-art suffering. He endured what he had to—appropriately, on God's terms. Even Job's wife wondered why, after such enormous heartbreaking problems, Job didn't "curse God and die." Job replied, "Though he [God] slay me, yet will I trust in him" (Job 13:15).

Wanderings, displacement of entire communities, have been a familiar trial for God's children since the beginning of time. Such an undertaking is a grand test because sacrifice and struggle of every kind are required.

Who will be valiant through such testing? Who will obey? Who will love God anyway and keep the faith? Who will gain precious experience needed for a higher level of eternal life? Who will become experienced enough to effectively help others in their tests?

Noah and his ark of sevens and pairs had to be ready to start the world again wherever they were when the floods subsided. Just because Noah was a prophet didn't make the task easy. His preparations were ridiculed and scoffed at.

Jared and his brother guided their people in strange barges they had built and then filled with seeds, fish, flocks, fowls of the air, and even swarms of honeybees. These barges were built with God's specific instruction—sealed "like unto a dish"—and ceaselessly "driven forth before the wind" to the promised land (Ether 2:17; 6:8). But there were mighty struggles to accomplish the escape from Babel.

Lehi with God's Liahona led his extended family and selected friends in an exodus from Jerusalem that was marked with trauma and suffering. Moses and the children of Israel were tried with all manner of suffering. Manna was their meal and new commandments shaped their lives. It was not easy.

And the Latter-day Saints' pioneer trek west was one of the most ambitious undertakings in the history of God's mobile children on earth. Again this organized migration from a people's familiar surroundings and homes was in response to

God's commandment. It was a mighty trial with a purpose. It was a program for adversity of every kind. The man held accountable before God for this mass movement was Brigham Young, who entered the valley ill with fever.

Mass migration is a mighty test. The upheaval of communities, the untimely and even violent death of loved ones, the discomfort and martyrdom, the loss of precious possessions and privacy, the vanished dreams for personal achievement, and stressful relationships were part of these migrations and the history of man up through our own time. Jews under Hitler, peasants in the time of the Czar, Cambodian refugees, black slaves, pilgrims, and many others across the earth have had to face this ultimate ordeal of mass migration.

The Lord has said: "My people must be tried in all things, that they may be prepared to receive the glory that I have for them, even the glory of Zion; and he that will not bear chastisement is not worthy of my kingdom" (D&C 136:31).

There it is: adversity is something we need to help prepare us to receive God's glory! There *are* blessings in disguise in adversity.

Adversity is something we need to respond to appropriately because it is part of life's preparation and proof of our obedience to God.

When we are hurting, when we are sick and suffering, when we feel weak-willed and discouraged, when our hearts are wrenched and depression and confusion are closing in, we should be on guard! As searchlights marking a path in the sky, as lights ablaze on an entertainment strip, or as whistles blowing, and sirens screeching—signals, attention getters—so trouble should signal to our mind, TEST! TRIAL! THINK! When the first sign of trouble, temptation, or testing comes into our life, the trained spirit within us shifts gears. We quicken our guard. All of our antennae are up. We check our fine-tuning.

"How must I respond so as to prove that I love the Lord anyway, and that I will not take up anger against him nor prove myself weak and untrustworthy?"

"What principle will help me now?"

"What am I to learn?"

"What do I need to know that I never dreamed I'd need to know?"

"After this experience, who needs the kind of help I now can give?"

When trouble comes, these are good questions to ask. I am not talking about simple nuisances or demands that are woven through daily life. I am talking about the kinds of trials that demand the best in us.

God becomes not only important but absolutely necessary to our survival and our learning through adversity. The Lord has said, "Pray always, and I will pour out my Spirit upon you, and great shall be your blessing—yea, even more than if you should obtain treasures of the earth."

And the next verse is a joyful verse! "Behold, canst thou read this without rejoicing and lifting up thy heart for gladness?" (D&C 19:38–39.)

God becomes not only important but also absolutely necessary to our spiritul growth. And to our joy. Shakespeare reminded us in *Much Ado About Nothing,* "How much better is it to weep at joy than to joy at weeping!"

Draw close to God, then, when your life and heart are burdened. Draw close to him, and he has promised to draw close to you. Adversity has blessings beneath its cloak, when you put your hand in the Lord's. And you can even become a witness to unexpected miracles.

We are troubled on every side,
yet not distressed;
we are perplexed,
but not in despair.

—2 Corinthians 4:8

8

Adversity and
the Miracle of Prayer

Through adversity we can come to know God, to love him, to value the plan and gift of life, to see his hand in our blessings.

Think of it this way: if we didn't suffer some, if we had everything that we wanted and most of what we needed without asking of Heavenly Father, we might drift away from God in our lives. Surely we wouldn't grow in our understanding that we are in debt to the Lord for all our blessings.

It is through adversity and the answers to our prayers that we become a witness to miracles in our time.

Adversity and the miracles wrought through fervent prayer because of that suffering is a blessing for people of all ages.

Tippy was the most precious possession in the life of our eight-year-old son. Tippy was a wiggling, lovable puppy with black, curly hair. But, unless our son Tony cuddled him, he yapped constantly. He was in a way like a newborn baby. I'd had six children in close marching order, and right then a yapping puppy was not number one on my list of priorities.

But Tony adored Tippy.

One day Tippy disappeared. We searched the neighborhood for him without success. No doubt someone had carried

this appealing black bundle off, I explained to Tony, and
added that maybe puppies weren't such a good idea on our
busy street anyway. I reasoned and comforted and tried to
pacify this precious son of ours with his favorite treats. But he
would not be changed in his determination to find Tippy.

"Mom, may I say my prayers early today?" he asked when
we reached home again after scouring the streets in our area.

"Of course, Tony. You may pray whenever you like, as
often as you like." I was tempted to take this teaching moment
and discourse on prayer to a ready eight-year-old but he
quickly interrupted me, "Will you come pray with me?"

Together we knelt by his bunk bed. My heart was warm
and tender at the little boy's outpourings, but it was fearful,
too. What if the puppy couldn't be found, couldn't find its
long way home after so short a time with us? Would Tony's
faith in Heavenly Father falter?

As it turned out, it was my faith that faltered. My need
wasn't as great perhaps. I would have forgotten about that
puppy and welcomed the peace from its yapping, except that
Tony wouldn't let me. We had an "extra" prayer each day
when he came home from school. Each prayer had as its sole
purpose the pleading with God to bless the puppy and bring
him home safely "some day." Tony was resolute.

Many days passed. One day I sent Tony out to the curb to
bring in the trash cans. Moments later he came bounding into
the house with the puppy in his arms. Tippy was an emaciated,
bedraggled dog with curled fur matted by dried blood. He'd
had some terrible adventure. All the way to the veterinarian we
cried tears of gladness and Tony kept repeating over and over,
"I knew Heavenly Father would bring Tippy back. I knew it!"

Oh, to be so positive about outcome to prayer! So tireless
in waiting for the Lord's timetable.

It was many weeks after this incident that I was giving a talk
in a neighboring stake Relief Society. I told about Tippy and
Tony's unfailing faith. The next day one of the women in that
meeting knocked on my door. She handed me a fat roll of her
famous caramel pecan candy. It seems that my story stirred a
memory in her, and she came with candy and a confession.
She said she was driving past our home one day near the

vacant lot and felt a thump. She didn't stop to check because she just assumed it was a piece of old tire or a stray cat as she saw the black object flip into the tall weeds of the vacant lot. She drove on her way. She was a woman in a hurry to a doctor's appointment.

Tippy had been injured seriously (indeed, the vet confirmed this) and apparently had been recuperating in the field while Tony's prayers were answered, keeping the dog alive. On that last day, Tippy had made his way as far as the trash cans when Tony found him.

In 2 Nephi 26:15 we are promised that "the prayers of the faithful shall be heard." My personal testimony is that this is so.

Mary had always enjoyed a close relationship with Heavenly Father and the Savior. She was a praying woman and a woman to whom gratitude was as natural as breathing. She had climbed mountains with the soul-testing experiences in her life, and because of the way she responded, she was honed into an exemplary woman.

Mary is in her nineties now, but life isn't over until it is over. Our tests aren't done until the last hour.

Mary is still being tested! She has been wracked with the anxiety, confusion, and sadness of change in life. One day she shared with me a choice experience that she had after a long period of pain, struggle, and sleepless nights.

"I had prayed many times before during this miserable period of my life. This time it was different. I was in a state of terrible mental confusion. I felt out of control. I was so needful and frantic that there was no help except God's help or I would surely be in the hands of the adversary!"

As the pressure built within Mary, she rushed to her bedside, fell upon her knees, and wailed out loud, "Oh, God, hear me! Hear my prayer. Give me peace!"

Her anguished cry echoed in her bedroom.

"Immediately, in the same instant that I cried out, I felt the evil confusion and darkness peel away from me. It started at the top of my head—in my brain where the frightening muddle had persisted—and it moved in an orderly manner right down my body and out my feet! You have seen those keys that you twist around a can of meat to open it, it was like that with me then. The consuming darkness came peeling off of me, and out of me, from head to toe, leaving my spirit and my body refreshed."

Then Mary added, "Can you imagine my deep gratitude to my Heavenly Father? I know he cares about me!"

We talked about how easy it can be to get out of control because of burdens. Mary's testimony is that when we lay our life in the lap of God, when we are truly brokenhearted and contrite, God grants us answers to our prayers.

"We are like Abraham," Mary explained. "He had to go to the full limit of the test, and then, only then, did God intervene." God's purposes and his timetable for us are not always easily recognized by us. However, he does not forsake us. If we turn to him in prayer when adversity comes, we will know this.

President Ezra Taft Benson taught the congregation at Elder A. Theodore Tuttle's funeral that he might be healed. Fervent prayers of the Saints can make a difference, he continued, but then added the reminder that in all prayers for favors, we submit, saying, "Thy will be done." Whatever happens then, we are to be comforted knowing God's will can only be for the ultimate good.

Emerson wrote that "no man ever prayed heartily without learning something." That is an interesting phrase—to pray heartily. It is true that the more we pray the more we'll understand, especially if we do it heartily.

Not long ago a young woman and her mother kept an appointment with me at our home. Debbie was not married. She was of high school age and expecting a baby. It was a terrible heartbreak for the family. The sin was distressing, but there was conflict in what to do about this forthcoming infant. The mother's first choice was that the "father" be forced to marry Debbie. If that didn't work, she felt the child should be kept in the family—in spite of what people would think.

Debbie was a sensitive, bright young woman who had plans for her life. She wanted a temple marriage some day. She wanted an education so that she could be a good wife and mother. She realized that she had made a mistake more dreadful than she had ever before suspected. Now that she was caught in the problem, she was repentant and wanted to move forward with her life. She also felt very keenly about doing what was best for this baby.

We talked about marrying this young man and then preparing for a later sealing in the temple. She was sure that he wasn't someone with whom she wanted to share the rest of her life.

"Nonsense," argued the mother, "he can change."

"Maybe," I added. "But two wrongs don't necessarily make a right. In other words, marrying the wrong man simply because you had sinned with him is not necessarily a proper response to the problem." In this case, it seemed that it would not assure the infant a proper home and years of security.

The next thing we talked about was that a mistake of the flesh is no excuse for denying a spirit child of Heavenly Father (which would be assigned to inhabit the baby's body) the best possible environment to grow up in on earth. A spirit child of our Heavenly Father is precious. Personal sacrifice might be necessary on the part of both Debbie and her mother in order to allow this spirit child's growth and the fulfillment of God's purposes.

These were tough decisions. Abortion, of course, was out of the question, though it had been considered.

Cramming for help during such adversity isn't as wise as living each day to be ready for whatever test might come— including temptations. But it is better to "cram" than never to learn at all. At last Debbie and her mother agreed to take their problem before God. They would prepare themselves for prayer. We talked of a priesthood blessing, fasting, wrestling with themselves for forgiveness and wisdom, searching the scriptures. It is good to do what we ought to do before we ask the Lord for direction and for his Spirit.

We think of Oliver Cowdery and his desire to translate and his accompanying failure. It is the classic example for us all, as we consider that the Lord said to Oliver, "Study it out in your mind; then you must ask me if it be right, and if it is right I will cause that your bosom shall burn within you; therefore, you shall feel that it is right" (D&C 9:8).

I reminded Debbie and her mother of this system for getting guidance.

Some time later Debbie called for another appointment.

The baby had been born just days before, and she wanted to talk about it with me.

While she was in labor, both Debbie and her mother asked for and received an incredible priesthood blessing through their bishop. Then when the baby was born, the feeling came over both Debbie and her mother that it was absolutely right to give this child up for adoption. Her mother's agreeing with her was an additional answer to Debbie's prayers.

Debbie shared with me the sweet knowledge that came to her that there was some family being prepared especially for this child of her flesh and the spirit child of Heavenly Father. Now she understood! She felt a real sense of partnership with God.

The adoption agency described three different families to Debbie, without revealing names or locations. Two of the families left Debbie feeling blank or numb. But, she said, when the third family was barely mentioned, her heart began to pound. Her body tingled all over. She knew in her heart and in her mind that this baby, fresh from heaven, belonged in that family.

Debbie knew, too, that her repentance and sorrow before God was accepted. She felt forgiven. Heavenly Father filled her soul with peace. Mother was comforted, too.

Now, consider the other part of this growing problem of babies being born out of wedlock.

A young mother stood in fast meeting the day her adopted son was given a name and a father's blessing. She told the story of the unusual circumstances surrounding this baby's being given to them. Her husband was out of town at the time the baby was born and couldn't be reached. She had to make the decision on her own without his counsel. Her prayers to Heavenly Father were fervent. It wasn't just a decision that affected their family; it also affected the baby boy. When she brought the baby home and looked into the face of the tiny stranger, she prayed again that she might know for certain that this little spirit belonged in their family.

As she held the newborn a powerful spiritual moment comforted her. She suddenly knew that this child was meant to be theirs. "It was a direct and definite spiritual confirmation that he belonged with us," she said. "I did not need an angel to come down and tell me personally that this was so. I *knew* it within me, and I thank God for such a precious answer to prayer."

During the fast and testimony meeting in which the baby was blessed and named, this young mother said that this same welling up of the Spirit filled her as her husband prayed over the baby. It was a precious underscoring of her previous answer to prayer.

Such is the power of God.

If you have lived very long, you know that life hands a variety of challenges into our lives before our day is done. Included among the assaults with which we might wrestle are temptation, infidelity, discouragement, disappointment, rebellious children, quarrelsome neighbors, senility in a family member, financial disaster, a seesaw marriage, a challenging Church assignment, physical handicaps. It is impossible to tackle such testings without God's help and expect a successful outcome as well as personal growth.

It is small consolation that all God's children have troubles. People get flat tires, too, but when it is your own deflated wheel or your flooded basement, for example, you have to deal with it. So it is with other kinds of trials. That's why careful prayer is such a blessing—it is personal help of the loftiest kind.

Many of us have similar testings, yet solutions—like growth —must come individually.

Kanako was a beautiful young friend of mine from Japan. We asked her to give the closing prayer at one of the general women's meetings broadcast across the world from the Tabernacle on Temple Square. Kanako was studying temporarily in Salt Lake City, Utah. It was exciting for us to have her and, we thought, for her to have this unusual opportunity.

As the day of the meeting drew closer, Kanako became increasingly nervous. She even talked about backing out. There were many reasons. Being a Japanese woman, she felt strange to be performing in public. She was young and in a strange country. She suffered about representing her people in the general church setting. She was fearful that she would embarrass her family.

She even considered the possibility that she would faint right there on the podium before the world who would be watching on television!

The night of the meeting Kanako looked particularly lovely, dressed in her traditional Japanese ceremonial robes. We requested this dress to give an international flavor to the meeting. At the prayer meeting before the broadcast, I slipped my arm through hers to walk upstairs to the Tabernacle stand. She was trembling. She whispered in my ear her concerns. I assured her that the Lord would bless her in a manner appropriate for the occasion.

I knew that she had a strong testimony of the Savior. I knew that she was bright and could converse quite well in English. I felt certain that she could pray in public, so I relaxed about her and focused on my own responsibilities for public appearance at the meeting.

When the time came for Kanako to take her place at the pulpit, it was a beautiful moment. The Japanese people are so very deferential and gracious. She stood reverently with her head bowed. But then minutes passed when she stood silent, not starting the prayer. When at last she did speak, we couldn't understand the words, yet we felt a powerful spirit.

Weeks later I received a letter telling about the miracle of the prayer by Kanako. Someone had brought to the Tabernacle a Japanese woman who was investigating the gospel. When the woman saw Kanako and heard the prayer in her own tongue, the Spirit quickened her. It was an answer to her own personal prayer for a witness at this meeting that The Church of Jesus Christ of Latter-day Saints was true and was where she belonged.

Another woman told me of a different kind of experience with prayer and Heavenly Father. It, too, has a message for us as we consider adversity in our lives.

Linda and Ralph loved each other. They were young, and Ralph's career was moving along successfully. Their new home was empty of furniture but full of good spirit.

Then calamity struck. Ralph was diagnosed as having a critical disease and the prognosis was negative. The disease worked its destruction on his body swiftly, and Ralph suffered incredibly. Linda was bereft. She felt threatened and helpless. Ralph needed constant care and constant prayer just to get him through the agony. As Ralph would struggle to endure, Linda would inevitably fall to her knees by his bedside and pray for Ralph's strength. She prayed for greater wisdom in the attending physicians. She prayed most of all, over and over again, that the miracle of healing would happen. She always prayed for forgiveness for her own weaknesses and lack of sufficient faith to bring about the desired healing.

One night as she knelt there, she prayed out loud as they had done together each bedtime since their marriage. In the midst of Linda's pleadings to God, Ralph touched her arm and said weakly, "Honey, don't go through all of that, just pray that I can sleep through the night . . . just pray I can sleep."

Linda wept. Of course . . . take each thing a step at a time. Right now, Ralph just needed sleep and escape. Linda mellowed as she humbly asked Heavenly Father to help Ralph to sleep that night. Immediately Ralph drifted into a deep sleep. Linda was able to get some much needed rest, as well.

In the morning when Linda checked, Ralph was dead. He had passed away in his sleep. For him, it was the answer to prayer. For Linda it was an acceptable heartbreak because she was filled with that incredible gift of peace as she looked upon her husband in his final sleep.

She told me that she dropped to her knees by his bed again and placed herself and her life in God's hands. Then she thanked him fervently for the comforting witness of love from heaven that flooded her as she prayed.

Over the years I have gathered countless wonderful stories about prayer, God's closeness, people's being comforted even when things don't turn out the way they wanted, of miracles, of spiritual support during struggles, and of peace and hope and assurance.

One of the strongest influences in my life came when I was a seminary girl under the wise shepherding of William E. Berrett. I remember a lesson about Parley P. Pratt on a sea voyage. Things on the sailing vessel took a bad turn when the prevailing winds died down and the ship was stranded for days in an unusual calm. Supplies were running seriously short. Matters were getting desperate. At last, people came to Elder Pratt who was asleep on deck. They knew him to be a missionary, a man of God. They stirred him and begged him to ask God to make the winds blow.

Elder Pratt had the passengers kneel on deck while he prayed very simply, as a man of complete faith can do. He asked God to bless them with "patience until the wind blows."

At the dedication of the Denver Temple, one of the stake presidents went to great trouble to squeeze a place in the celestial room for a single girl with a serious problem. Space was tight because of the large choir and the television equipment. Only General Authorities, their wives, and certain local leaders were privileged to sit in that room.

But the stake president managed a place for Jenny. This young woman had suffered greatly most of her life. Her crippling and painful disease made her life miserable twenty-four hours a day. She had only one leg now, too. The pain in her arms made it impossible for her to use crutches. She lived with a father and an unmarried brother who took care of her, but in the temple she sat in a wheelchair, alone.

This story has an inspiring history. Jenny had been deeply discouraged until an idea struck her. The temple was to be dedicated, and that meant the prophet, President Ezra Taft Benson, would be there. If she could just touch him, she would be made well. She knew it! She didn't ask for a blessing. She would pray to God that she would somehow be able to touch the prophet, and then she would be free of pain. That's why she had to sit in the celestial room at the dedication, so that she could be near President Benson.

President Benson knew nothing of the young woman or her plans. On the day of dedication Jenny sat in her place in the celestial room waiting for the General Authorities to come in for the meeting. Jenny suddenly was filled with an exhilarating sweetness and lift of spirit. She looked around. President Benson was coming along the aisle where she sat. As he passed her place, Jenny reached out an aching arm and touched

President Benson. Immediately she felt healing powers in her body.

"I haven't had a moment's pain since then," Jenny affirmed. "Now I can walk with crutches. God loves me. He loves me, and he hears and answers prayers!"

This incident reminds me of a similar one that happened with my own husband when he was a missionary in the Hawaiian Islands. He was called to a home where a little son was desperately ill and plagued with a very high temperature. The parents despaired but the boy was certain that if he could hold my missionary husband's Bible next to his body he would be made well. Jim left the Bible with the boy who slept with it. The next day the Bible was returned with the good news that the boy was healed.

Some years ago I sat in a sacred testimony meeting in the Tabernacle with a select group of LDS college students. Several General Authorities were there, too, as well as leaders from some of the areas of the Church that the student delegates represented at this convention.

One of the speakers was a man from California who told of the day his wife called him at work, frantically reporting that their family home was threatened. The winds had changed and the flames from a fierce canyon fire had driven people from their homes. Police had put up a barricade.

Richard left at once for the street where his home was threatened. He broke through the police blockade. He raced toward his house noting that other homes up and down the street were already in flames. The landscaping about his property was on fire already. Richard took the garden hose and tried to put out the flames, but the fire was too strong. He took the garden hose and climbed to the roof, wetting the area down as he went. It was no use. The fire was too much for a single garden hose.

But it was not too much for the power of God!

Richard remembered this as he dropped the hose. For a moment he thought of the great recreation his ward members enjoyed in their home. It was the only fun in many lives pressured with little income and much struggle as they studied at the university. Richard was the bishop of that ward and his spacious home was an oasis for his needful ward members. He talked this over with the Lord in those tense moments on the roof. He didn't need the home for himself and his wife. He needed it for the people in his ward. It would be a witness that God was mindful of them if the house could be saved.

Richard then raised his arm to the square, and through the power of the priesthood of God which he holds, and in the name of Jesus Christ, Richard blessed the house against the encroaching flames and all other destructive elements.

Richard's home was only scorched while other homes burned on that street of devastation. He weeps when he thinks of God's attention to details and to the needs of simple people in a small dot of a place on all the earth.

The press reported the miracle and a public witness of Christ changed many lives.

Years ago a certain class in the Church was discussing the handcart phase of the pioneer movement. There was much criticism expressed against those early Church leaders for allowing people to move west so ill-equipped so late in the season of storms.

As the class members warmed to the subject and the spirit of the meeting turned negative, an old gentleman, who had kept his silence until he could stand it no longer, stood and courageously chastised the group. He told them that they were wrong to speak so freely of things they knew nothing about. He admitted that there were mistakes in judgment and that people suffered and died in great numbers because of that. But that wasn't the entire story, according to him.

He said in essence, "I was in that handcart company. My wife was in it, too. We suffered beyond anything you can imagine in starvation and exposure and exhaustion. But tell me, did you ever hear a survivor of that company utter a word of criticism? Not one of that company ever apostatized or left the Church, because every one of us came through with the absolute knowledge that God lives. We became acquainted with him in our extremities."

His outburst continued: "I have pulled my handcart when I was so weak and weary from illness and lack of food that I could hardly put one foot in front of the other. I have looked ahead and seen a patch of sand or a slope and I have said, 'I can only go that far and there I must give up.' But when I reached it, the cart began pushing me. I knew that the angels of God were there. Am I sorry that I chose to come with that handcart company in that season? No! Neither then nor any minute of my life since. The price we paid to become acquainted with God was a privilege to pay." (This story was recorded in the Relief Society lessons included in the January 1948 issue of the Relief Society Magazine, page 8.)

I love that story. I have heard this same kind of testimony from people who have endured public disgrace, excommunication, terrible struggles with health, personal hurt, spiritual slack, deprivation, or even torture and abuse. All across the earth we hear stories of trials that have been solved or withstood with the help of God and through application of his principles. And the wonder of it is that great or small miracles do come in the wake of adversity.

Do you recall these fine lines from *The Rime of the Ancient Mariner,* by Samuel Taylor Coleridge?

> He prayeth well who loveth well
> Both man and bird and beast.
> He prayeth best who loveth best
> All things both great and small.
> For the dear God who loveth us,
> He made and loveth all.

This we believe, that God lives and loves us and will help us. But even so is it ever all right to cry?

I will control myself,
Or go inside.
I will not flaw perfection
with my grief.
Handsome, this day:
No matter who has died.

—Edna St. Vincent Millay

9

Adversity and the Weeping Eye

Many tears are shed during adversity, and considering the amount of adversity in the world today, that is a lot of water.

Like Jeremiah lamenting the miserable estate of Jerusalem, there was a time when I was lamenting the miserable state of my life at that time. That meant tears. And a lot of good tears are.

One day, I consulted the scriptures for a Primary lesson I was preparing and came across Lamentations 3:26, which says: "It is good that a man should both hope and quietly wait for the salvation of the Lord." I vaguely wondered if that counsel applied to women, too.

You see, I was the wife of a new bishop, the young mother of many. To help with the family finances, I wrote a daily newspaper column and had a weekly television show. Life was full and pushing around me. My husband, it seemed to me, was always gone. To sit and wait for the salvation of the Lord to get me out from under the burdens that tried my strength, spirit, and wit, seemed too much to ask of God.

I needed help; there was no doubt about that. I was certain God *could* help, but I was not certain that he *would* or even that he *should*. I felt hopeless. I was on a treadmill with my legs getting shorter and my breathing turning into gasps.

There was a lot of self-pity, too, and one day I was wallowing in it. I contemplated making a double chocolate cake and not giving any to the children until I had eaten my full. I was looking up the recipe when there came a gentle rapping at my door.

Janet was there, my dear friend who taught at the university. She had stolen a moment between classes to visit me. Her own little ones were being cared for at home by a husband sorely stricken with arthritis and unable to work any longer. It was midmorning, and a visit at this hour of the day was most unusual. Surely she was sent on a ministering angel's errand, for I was in the depths. I needed a new way of looking at my own troubles for a moment, then, according to her words, I'd be able to "pick up my wagon handle again and head west!"

I welcomed her with joy, but she couldn't come in. She merely handed me help on a scrap of paper and went back to her car. I looked at the message in my hand. It was just a "Peanuts" cartoon with the Charlie Brown crowd. And I had hoped for hope, comfort!

Then I read the dialogue . . . and caught her message.

Lucy had set up a packing box as her "psycho shop." Most kids use such a setup to sell lemonade, but Lucy was selling psychiatric counsel for five cents. The sign announced that the "doctor" was in.

Charlie Brown approached. He explained that he wanted to be liked, even admired. He wanted to be the life of every party and the hope of every person. When he asked Lucy if she understood these desires, she said she understood perfectly. Then she added, "Forget it!" (See Charles M. Schulz, "Peanuts Treasury" [New York: Holt, Rinehart, and Winston, 1968], p. 13.)

This precious perspective my friend shared with me was a reminder not to take myself and my problems too seriously. Forget it—for the time being laugh and forget self.

While laughter is good medicine for the moment, life is mostly very serious business. We can't exactly giggle through it with any sense of reality or responsibility. But preoccupation with our own view of life can smother hope. Self-pity can stifle wisdom. Easy tears, as these poetic lines affirm, can blind perspective:

> Weep not! beloved, for that rush of tears
> Is like a liquid veil upon thine eyes.
> What matter if another dawn brings sighs
> Another hostile day its press of fears.
> Weep not, a weeping eye can never see
> How great a web of comfort may be drawn
> Out of another heart into thine own
> Nor even my two hands stretched out to thee.
> What if the dawn that web of comfort break,
> Mock at the dawn, beloved, for my sake.

—W. B. Yeats (from *Ah, Sweet Dancer* [New York: The Macmillan Company, 1971], p. 134)

So we dry our eyes and we get on with life, no matter what it holds for us each day.

One of the quickest ways out of the doldrums is to consider with whom you'd trade places when it comes to trouble. Everybody these days seems to have a mighty portion of it, whether by their own making or from something beyond their control.

You stop weeping for yourself when you consider the plight of some people. Here are some lines to awaken your best perspective:

> Blessed are they who understand
> My faltering step and palsied hand.
> Blessed are they who know that my ears today
> Must strain to catch the things they say.
> Blessed are they who seem to know
> That my eyes are dim and my wits are slow.
> Blessed are they with a cheery smile
> Who stop to chat for a little while.
> Blessed are they who never say,
> "You've told that story twice today."
> Blessed are they who make it known
> That I'm loved, respected, and not alone.

Blessed are they who know I'm at loss
To find the strength to carry the Cross.
Blessed are they who ease the days
Of my journey Home in loving ways.
                              —Esther Mary Walker

While I was serving as general president of the Young Women, I received an anonymous note with a crisp twenty-dollar bill enclosed. In the letter a woman confessed that she'd stolen that amount from the cash box when she was at a Young Women's girls camp twenty years ago. She had suffered all these years from that dishonest act. Every time she went in for a temple recommend interview she worried and wept. She felt unworthy, though she kept her problem to herself and got her recommend.

One day she read something President Spencer W. Kimball had written about repentance and forgiveness and peace. Suddenly she saw things in a different light. There was a way out. She didn't need to cry inside any more and fear the future. She could do something about it.

Her problem was a special kind of nagging that got worse as she learned more about the gospel and wanted to live more exactly, resolving all problems according to the Lord's will.

The harder we try to be good, to be like Christ, the clearer our faults can seem to us. This good sister decided to tackle her problem—to not fret over it any longer. She found a way to wipe out self-destructive behavior and get on with her life.

Another woman, following the untimely death of her husband, called our office for an appointment with me. She was grieving over her loss. But it wasn't just loneliness that brought her tears to the point of despair; it was the thought that she might not be worthy of joining her beloved partner in the next world.

She repeatedly prayed for help. At last, she resolved to quit crying and to prepare herself for the day of reunion. Her preparation included righting every wrong.

As we talked and wept together, she expressed the details of an old problem. Years ago she had been untruthful about earning a special award in one of the Church programs for young women. She came to my office to return the award. The burden of separation from her husband was lightened as she took positive action by examining her life and preparing herself for life after death.

The death of a husband is a sorrowful, personal experience. There are tears indeed at such a time. But there are ways to sublimate the feelings that arise from such a separation or to take the sting out of it. Even the passage of time can blunt death's sharp edges, but ultimately only reunion can fully assuage it. So, more than mere comfort is needed when eyes brim with tears during this ultimate test of loneliness. The following examples show how some women found the peace they needed.

"My world seemed shattered when my husband died suddenly in his sleep," recalled Sister Elva Cowley. "I had always loved the outdoors. But even on a sunny day the sky seemed dim to me after he died. I'd look at people and wonder how they could walk down the street smiling."

She wept and grieved for months and at last accepted a position as a receptionist at the Primary Children's Hospital. That was the beginning of finding joy in life again. She compared her own lot with the trouble of others. And in that hospital there is adversity enough to dry anyone's tears.

"Some people can take trouble," she explained. "Some people learn lessons from these experiences and press on. But some folks just buckle under. I was buckling under until the day a young mother came into the hospital with the most pitifully deformed baby I had ever seen. I was amazed that she was in such good spirits. I asked her how she managed such a trial."

"She replied, 'I know that my Heavenly Father loves me because he knew that he could send this little spirit to me and that I would really love it and care for it.' "

Sister Cowley continued, "That was the day I saw with new eyes. I began counting my store of blessings that proved Heavenly Father loved me, too. I knew that I must not give in to the negativism that Satan tempts us with."

Weeping can endure for a time, but when tears and self-pity are prolonged, we are targets for greater trouble. Our progress is hampered.

Some months after the death of Elder Richard L. Evans of the Quorum of the Twelve Apostles, I visited with his wife, Alice. I wanted to know how she was getting along without her husband and the lovely experiences they had enjoyed in their position in the Church.

"Let me read to you from Ether 12:6," responded Sister Evans. She opened an impressively worn Book of Mormon and read, " 'Wherefore, dispute not because ye see not, for ye receive no witness until after the trial of your faith.' Losing the husband you've loved for so long is the ultimate trial of one's faith, I now know. This matter of faith is all you have to fall back on at such a time. We've taught our four sons the importance of abiding faith. I've given little talks and shared my testimony about faith. Then, out of the blue, my big test came with Richard's death. The most helpful thing in this tremendously difficult period of adjustment has been my sure knowledge that Richard, like Christ, lives! I don't know what people do without this faith."

A General Authority and his wife are in a position to see that people have problems—even people who look as if they have the world by the proverbial tail. So Sister Alice Evans spends a good part of her time sharing her marvelous warmth and goodness in careful concern for people with problems, especially widows and single women. "When I think of the circle of love I've lived in," comments Sister Evans, "and compare my loneliness now to that of the older, unmarried woman, I know that her problem is worse than mine. I suppose there are many ways we have our faith tested. It is up to each of us to meet that trial of our faith."

Another sister, Barbara, was a physical education major looking forward to a career as a teacher. The summer before her senior year at the university she was injured in an automobile accident, which left her paralyzed from the waist down.

Barbara was faithful, inevitably faithful, in her life. That's the kind of girl she had always been. This, of course, was her first experience with severe adversity. But she was undaunted. Family prayers and personal prayers to God, whom she knew lived and loved her, would be answered. She'd get well. She was a determined and a cooperative patient. But faith brought only dashed dreams. All the blessings, therapy and treatment had readied her, at best, only for life in a wheelchair.

One day, alone in her hospital room, she quietly pleaded with God that in the therapy session that afternoon she would feel something—some sign of healing.

A deep darkness crowded her heart. Suddenly she knew she was not going to be whole after all. The tears came, the weakness of spirit, the desperate need for comfort and understanding, the overwhelming emotion that she would rather be dead.

Then, long minutes after giving in to despair, Barbara wailed inside herself, "Oh, God, dear Heavenly Father. Help me! Help me to take this terrible tragedy. Thy will be done."

She no longer said, "Help me to walk." Barbara placed herself totally in God's hands, her inner will succumbing to his greater knowledge of her life. Then came the sweetness of the Spirit welling up within her.

Barbara's change in attitude was not simply resigning to the inevitable; it was submitting willingly to God. "Thy will be done" is an attitude of supreme faith, saying that whatever God wanted for her was what she wanted, too. She would be all right. She could do it. She wasn't alone.

Her faith and acceptance didn't take the course of placid resignation. She made plans. And those plans included being a kind of ministering angel to other patients with similar problems but without her kind of faith.

She's gone on to become a superb servant in the work of the Lord. She's also completed a doctorate in her chosen field of health and physical education. She is a popular teacher and public speaker.

And she could have merely wiped her weeping eyes again and again.

Maggie's divorce wasn't what she had in mind. Neither was her husband's faithlessness. Maggie's struggle to be Christlike through her struggle required much soul- and scripture-searching.

When they married in the temple, Maggie was sure that she and Todd would be together forever. Later, his actions and the excommunication that followed seemed to wipe any remembrance from Todd's mind of their goals and covenants. Maggie wanted to forgive and forget and to try again. Todd insisted on a divorce.

It was done. It was humiliating and heartbreaking and devastating in countless ways. Her personal rejection was heightened by the fact that the "other woman" was her neighbor, who was bearing Todd's child.

Details are tiresome—the story is such a familiar one these days. But what makes Maggie's story worth talking about in a book on adversity is what she did about what happened to her.

What she did was to hide the tears and embark on a plan to turn a burden into a blessing. It was her only avenue to survival, let alone happiness. With God's help she set about implementing her plan. She'd solve life's problems according to God's principles.

First, she needed a lifting attitude, an idea to cling to that would chase the blues away. She decided to have a wonderful dinner party with the theme "I'm Free Again." (As if such freedom were what she wanted all the time!)

Second, she needed people around her who understood. She made up a guest list of other young mothers who had been abandoned by adulterous husbands. They were women who loved the Lord, who loved the gospel, and who lived it.

Third, she needed a perspective on her life so that she wouldn't make the same mistakes again.

At the dinner a linen handkerchief marked each place. Maggie explained the theme: "I'm Free Again!" She also talked about the goals the group might set. The handkerchief was the mood-maker. It was to be used to wave a salute to freedom for another chance and a better life. They'd all learned something through their heartbreak. They could wave a handkerchief in a fun gesture of celebration.

If some wanted to use the handkerchief to cry on, so be it; they must, however, do it on their own time. They all had been rejected. They all had wept over dashed dreams. A rehash of the details of sordid struggles wasn't what anyone needed now.

This was a blessing-counting occasion and a time to look forward.

They discussed a plan to grow on. The plan included getting skilled help for their particular kinds of problems—single parenting, financial planning, legal rights. But more than that, they wanted spiritual help. They were in a position to wonder about the Lord's purposes for them and their little children. They wanted to know more about what the Church provided and the gospel promised. They wanted their values shored up so that there wouldn't be a rebound into another poor situation.

It was a turning point for many of them. Over the months they carried out plans of learning, and they enjoyed compatible company with new friends who understood.

This companionship kept them growing, pressing toward the ultimate eternal goal. They kept up on personal appeal and in time, each woman married a fine new husband!

Another trial that might cause us to weep is a forced move. Breaking up a family home usually breaks somebody's heart. So much that has meant security, tradition, identity, and happiness is sifted, sorted, boxed up, portioned off, or cast away. Tears are shed as memories surface. Traumatic decisions must be made.

What can be the blessing behind this kind of adversity? Where can comfort come in such a threatening change? What attitude or course of behavior can dry the weeping eye?

Financial disaster wiped out the resources of our family. We were forced to move from our three-story home to an apartment. Conditions would be crowded at best, so we couldn't take most of our belongings.

Years of family growing, celebrating, serving, studying, and acquiring cluttered each room and storage place. We now had to make decisions about every item.

After a family counsel—a prayer and a rehearsal of God's ultimate purpose for his children—we decided that instead of having a commercial yard sale, we would share the things we couldn't use—the treasures as well as the "precious trash." In our time of unhappiness, we could bring delight to others.

We held a come-and-get-it affair. We did it in style, too. The dining room table was spread with the best cloth, baked pastries, and lemonade. Blossoms from the garden banked the entrance hall. It was a festive time.

Neighbors, close friends, and extended family members of all ages were invited to wander through the various bedrooms to see displays of the items to be given away. Guests could choose to take whatever they wanted! Books and records were available in the library. Games and hobby equipment were found in the family room. And so it went, all through the house.

Of course, people were startled—almost disbelieving—at first. But soon it was fun—and a very practical solution to our problem. People not only left that family home laden with gifts but they also had an idea of what one might do about certain kinds of adversity in order to turn tears into joy. It was a time of remembering God's goodness, too, and it was a time of heartwarming exchange. This had been a happy home where good lessons were learned right up to the last day. "Out of the abundance of the heart," indeed!

Severe trouble tends to underscore the kind of relating people engage in. Our family was active in the Church. We supported each other in Church-related duties as well as in those chores about the house or in the community that were required of us. We loved each other and when trouble came we were bound even more closely together. Of course, everyone felt brokenhearted about leaving the family home. Admittedly tears came easily until we hit upon our plan to bring joy to others. That plan turned the whole experience around. The remarkable thing is that down the road several years, what had seemed a terrible burden and disappointment (breaking up and leaving behind our family home), proved to be a powerful preparation for other more challenging experiences family members later faced.

Rather than just shedding tears, strive for gratitude—for a chance to grow closer to God, to prove worthy of his trust, to learn lessons that can help us help others. This should be our attitude and goal. Yes, this is more easily said than done, especially at first, but with proper practice we can become good at flourishing under adversity.

The letter that follows was sent to me a few months ago. I had given a talk at a multistake gathering and used this scripture: "And I will encircle thee in the arms of my love. Behold, I am Jesus Christ, the Son of God." (D&C 6:20–21.) A gentleman in the audience was touched by it because of a sacred experience he had had a year before. Hearing a scripture describe what happened to him prompted his letter in which he shared the details of an answer to prayer. It might help you.

"About a year ago . . . my wife and I had become deeply weighed down in spirit because of our financial struggles. I remember asking in my prayers for the strength and comfort to continue through the rough times. I shed tears of grief and frustration. I begged for relief at the hand of Heavenly Father.

"One night in prayer, my heart felt overwhelmed with the cares and burdens of my world, and I saw no end in sight. As I lay sleeping, someone entered my bedroom and, calling me from the bed, told me that I was to receive added responsibilities in Church work, and that I was to have an interview in the temple before the work could be given to me.

"Momentarily, I found myself standing within a room (in which temple it was, I don't know, but I was admiring the decor). I had a feeling of apprehension, as one always does before an interview. My back was to the door of the room. While I was thus waiting, the door behind me opened, and at that moment I became conscious of the fact that I could spiritually discern, or see, everything and in every direction within the room, even though I had not physically moved.

"The Personage who stood in the doorway radiated love and warmth and light, so much so that it filled the room and permeated every fiber of my being. His very Presence testified. I knew both body and spirit, both mind and heart, that I stood in the presence of my Savior and Redeemer, Jesus Christ.

"I was so overwhelmed by the power of His love that I could do no more than just stand where I was and weep. I had not the strength to move.

"I saw Him! With my spiritual eyes I saw Him!

"He made His way across the room to me. No words were uttered. No words were needed. He came up to me, and from behind, encircled me in a loving embrace. I will never forget the touch of His arms around me, nor the press of His embrace.

"Then the moment was over, the interview ended. I found myself in bed again, crying silently to myself.

"For weeks afterwards, even a casual thought of this sacred experience brought great tears to my eyes and I would remember His love. I would be overwhelmed for a time again.

"I wish I could say the terrible trials ended then. They didn't. In fact, things got worse. But the point is, it doesn't matter. *It doesn't matter!* Because I would go wherever He called me, suffer whatever He gave me in the way of chastisement, growth, changes, or hardships, knowing that He is with me and loves me. That knowledge eases the burdens. It doesn't take them away (and I have never asked to have trials taken away altogether), but my heart is eased and my mind at peace. I can suffer the troubles with cheerfulness and gratitude.

"I am still the same man—just an ordinary man. God has seen fit to answer my prayers and honor our fasting. He has given me a gift beyond price or measure. He will give the same gift to anyone who needs and seeks it properly. I so testify."

In Isaiah 30:20–21 is the following counsel: "And though the Lord give you the bread of adversity, and the water of affliction, yet shall not thy teachers be removed into a corner any more, but thine eyes shall see thy teachers: And thine ears shall hear a word behind thee, saying, This is the way, walk ye in it."

This kind of counsel has a way of drying the weeping eye so that we can see God's purposes more clearly. In the midst of affliction we can move forward, finding a solution to our problems, or developing an attitude and endurance that echoes our faith.

The idea is to keep from making
bigger problems.

10

In the Midst
of Affliction

Life is school. As Emerson said, "This time like all times is a good one if we but learn what to do with it."

If it is our time and turn to be tested, the best thing we can do is learn from it. An attitude of learning helps us to remember that in the midst of affliction our table is spread and our cup runneth o'er (see "The Lord Is My Shepherd," *Hymns,* 1985, no. 108). We can remember that no matter how bad things get, others have had worse trials. And we can remember how greatly we have been blessed by Heavenly Father. We know these things, of course, but remembering them in times of trial brings comfort and an awareness of God's goodness. If while in the midst of our suffering we can count our blessings, the healing can begin.

Sister Freda Joan Lee and I stood with our arms about each other the morning after her husband, President Harold B. Lee, passed away. It was the season of Christmas 1973. Sister Lee sobbed and said, "The world is mourning a prophet, but I have lost my husband. And I have had him such a short time."

Sister Lee, since then deceased herself, was in her sixties when she married President Lee, following the death of his first wife, and she comforted countless numbers of single girls with this hope. Thinking of separation now, plus a stretch of loneliness ahead proved a consuming trial for her. She who had comforted so many now stood on the uncomfortable threshold of despair herself.

Later, lonely and struggling to understand the untimely death of her husband who had been President of the Church for a brief eighteen months, Sister Lee sat in church on the back bench. She had a prayer in her heart for peace. In the midst of her affliction she turned to God for a way back up and out of anguish.

Then the closing song was sung. It was "Though Deepening Trials" by Eliza R. Snow. The last verse particularly comforted her:

> Lift up your hearts in praise to God;
> Let your rejoicings never cease.
> Though tribulations rage abroad,
> Christ says, "In me ye shall have peace."
> (*Hymns,* 1985, p. 122.)

"By the time we sang that last verse," said Sister Lee, "a wonderful lifting assurance had welled up within me. I was at peace. The Comforter had come. All would be well."

Another hymn, a new one, written and composed by Emma Lou Thayne and Joleen G. Meredith, soothes sorrowing souls. I recommend it for anyone needing comfort or guidance.

> Where can I turn for peace? Where is my solace
> When other sources cease to make me whole?
> When with a wounded heart, anger, or malice,
> I draw myself apart, Searching my soul?

> Where, when my aching grows, Where, when I languish,
> Where, in my need to know, where can I run?
> Where is the quiet hand to calm my anguish?
> Who, who can understand? He, only One.

> He answers privately, Reaches my reaching
> In my Gethsemane, Savior and Friend.

Gentle the peace he finds for my beseeching.
Constant he is and kind, Love without end.
("Where Can I Turn for Peace, *Hymns,* 1985, no. 129.)

I have interviewed countless people in the times of their adversities. Whatever they seem to be at first glance, the fact is, that when they are in the midst of affliction, the human spirit usually rises to blessed heights. Their innate goodness and strength can be further enhanced as they apply gospel principles to trying situations and as they keep close to the Lord. Then the light of the Lord seems to permeate their being.

Whatever the details of your life may be, your personal joy can yet be full. The principles of the gospel applied to tests in your life prepares the way for greater blessings.

Good can come from trouble.

Trauma can enliven the heart and enrich the soul. Clouds do have silver linings, and the leaf will burst again on the dry branch.

To you who are young, so attractive and hopeful; to you wise and wonderful ones who have lived longer and suffered more; to you with many dreams and to you whose dreams have already been dashed; to you who have given way to the temptings unleashed upon us all; to you stricken ill; to you whose faith has faltered and whose tears have washed the cheeks of a loved one or secretly dampened the pillow at night —to all of you, I say, "Seek to know that Heavenly Father and the Lord Jesus Christ live and sustain us."

But first the testing—the bitter so that we can value the sweet. First the trial—then the witness of our faith.

The scriptures support this truth.

> Who shall separate us from the love of Christ? shall tribulation, or distress, or persecution, or famine, or nakedness, or peril, or sword?
>
> For I am persuaded, that neither death, nor life, nor angels, nor principalities, nor powers, nor things present, nor things to come, Nor height, nor depth, nor any other creature, shall be able to separate us from the love of God, which is in Christ Jesus our Lord. (Romans 8:35, 38–39.)

Father Abraham in describing the creation of the world told us that God said, "And we will prove them herewith, to see if they will do all things whatsoever the Lord their God shall command them" (Abraham 3:25).

We are tested to see if God can trust us. We are tested that we may gain experience and be far more compassionate and effective in helping others, in doing the work of the Lord. We are tested that we may draw close to God and know that he is.

The history of mankind and, more specifically, the history of the Saints is a library full of remarkable stories of suffering in body and spirit. But they are also stories of triumph of the soul. Survival and richness of spirit come as God visits his children in their afflictions.

Stories of wars, holocausts, mass migrations, depression, revolutions and rebellions, plagues, illnesses, human emotion out of control between people, disasters of nature, and impositions of governments—all these stories of people's trials are also stories of their triumphs. Even in today's period of moral decay and terrorism, there are thrilling accounts of people turning to God for help in humble faith and of his goodness in return.

We can be blessed not in spite of nagging tests in life, but because of them. Fortunate are those who, in whatever period of time or trial, try to live by the word of God and not by the precepts or trends of men.

Life, after all, isn't only trouble. In the midst of affliction we are burdened, if you will, with great blessings. If you try counting blessings you will quickly see how easily they outnumber trials.

Painful things of life, after they are tucked away resolved, can be gathered forth to guide you in future times of trial or to help someone else undergoing adversity.

As we counsel with the Lord in all our doings, we will know that in the midst of affliction our table truly is spread. We will sense new power. We will know comfort no matter how severe our tribulations are at the moment.

Perhaps we are now ready to consider some practical steps in turning our burdens into blessings.

We are but warriors for the working-day;

Our gayness and our gilt
are all besmircht

With rainy marching
in the painful field;

There's not a piece of
feather in our host . . .

And time hath worn us
into slovenry:

But, by the mass, our
hearts are in the trim.

—Shakespeare
King Henry the Fifth

11

How to Turn Burdens Into Blessings

.

In the first chapter we discussed that through faulty behavior or lack of understanding we can turn blessings in life into burdens. Now, let's turn it around—by living the gospel we can turn adversity or burdens into blessings.

There is a novelty bookmark for sale these days which features Garfield, the smart-alec cat. The inscription suggests, "Read the ending first. Life is so uncertain."

As uncertain as life is, there are some things we can count on—trouble, trials, tests, tribulations, disaster, heartache, sin, and adversity. At times we stumble, make mistakes, bleed, hurt, agonize, berate ourselves, lash out at others. Though errors are part of being human we still suffer. At other times we are quietly going about our business and burdens are dumped on us.

It helps to remember that "this life is the time to prepare to meet God" (Alma 34:32), and we are rapidly becoming what we are going to be. So, if a burden comes, it is to our important advantage to turn it into a blessing somehow. If we have a plan to deal with trouble in a winning way, no trouble will be all that bad, in the end.

When all the philosophizing is finished, when all the sermons have been preached, when all the psychologists have had their say, we are still left to respond by ourselves to what is happening to us at any given moment of crisis. Depending upon a number of factors, our dealing with adversity can benefit us.

But we need a plan. Here are some tried and true ways to turn burdens into blessings. They are part of the gospel of Jesus Christ, and they can form the basis of such a plan for you: Pray; study the scriptures and find which of the gospel laws irrevocably decreed will help; bridle your passions by practicing self-control; repent by examining your life and putting it in order before seeking God's forgiveness; take charge of your life by developing compassion for others but demand more of yourself; seek truth in order to flourish; count your many, many blessings.

Pray

When adversity in any form hits, pray. Usually we think of prayer in the life and death traumas. But small problems can become bigger ones if we haven't made a practice of turning first to Heavenly Father for whatever it takes to solve, survive, and deal appropriately with our challenge at the moment.

Prayer is a great blessing.

When I was a little girl, a young couple moved into our ward and opened up a new world for me. They sang duets. I thought their singing together was wonderfully romantic, so I listened intently to their music. One of my favorite numbers was their version of "I Walked in the Garden Alone." To me, none have sung that old Christian heart-warmer as well as J. Stuart and Clara McMaster. I learned then that earnest prayer can be a song of the heart.

For years my brother Aldon and I tried to imitate the McMasters with that song. We'd harmonize all the way to wherever and back. Being scrunched all together in the family car wasn't as miserable when we sang.

The chorus went something like this:

> And He walks with me,
> And He talks with me,

And He tells me I am His own.
And the joy we share
As we tarry there
None other has ever known.

My brother and I still harmonize on this simple prayer in song, even though we are anything but children now. Our voices have changed, of course. And so have our prayers. Even the love of God seems different—it is more marvelous to me now than it was long ago when I didn't truly understand. I've been through some things since childhood, and I've come to value the magnificence of God's love.

I wonder how people manage life without taking their burdens to the Lord. He may not give us immediate relief from the problem we're struggling with, but we can get a lift in spirit. We can sense direction. We can feel God's love. We can be greatly strengthened. We can be aware of his sustaining influence. We can be heartened to go forward.

If you are burdened, pray. You will feel comforted.

If you are dying, pray. You will have peace.

If your husband goes off with another woman, pray. Pray for comfort, for guidance, for patience, for forgiveness, and the soul will heal.

If your teenager is in desperate trouble with drugs, sex, dishonesty, rebellion, or grades, pray. You'll know that God cares. He'll sustain you in your efforts to help the troubled youth.

If you lose your job and the bills are piled high, pray. Pray until your faith is firm. Then your mind is ready to receive God's will.

If you are depressed and hopeless, pray. Hope is the other side of faith. Pray, and know that God lives. Everything will ultimately be all right.

Even Cary Grant, a Hollywood star who seemingly had everything, believed in prayer. He once said, "If you don't have faith, pray anyway. If you don't understand or believe the words you're saying, pray anyway. Prayer can start faith, particularly if you pray aloud. And even the most imperfect prayer is an attempt to reach God."

Read again in 1 Samuel 1 about Hannah's fasting and praying in the temple so that she could have a child. Read again Mormon 5:2 about the foolish people who "did struggle for their lives *without* calling upon that Being who created them" (italics added).

Don't struggle aimlessly—pray!

God will hear your prayers, and you will know that he has heard.

Now, that's a blessing. With all the troubles any one of us has in a lifetime, we should think of the blessings that will be ours if we turn to heaven for help. Don't forget the promises regarding prayer. The scriptures are full of them. Here are a few that refer particularly to praying about problems: Matthew 5:44; Alma 13:28; 37:37; Moroni 7:48; D&C 9:8; 98:1–3; 112:10.

Remember, however, that while nothing is impossible with God, faith without works is dead. Part of solving any problem —even with prayer—is to do something about it yourself. Don't leave everything up to God. Study the word of God as contained in the scriptures and as revealed through his ordained servants. Prepare yourself now to act in wisdom.

Study the Scriptures

Danny was a fine man I met on a Church assignment. On the ride to the stake center he and his second wife, Anna, each bore witness to the value of scripture study in their lives.

Anna had filled a mission. The years passed, and she thought she would never marry. She suffered the accompanying heartbreak that often comes. She was tender as she spoke of keeping close to the Lord and maintaining a seeking, positive spirit through daily study of the scriptures. Finally, when eternal purposes and earthly timetables were right, she met Danny.

"I wouldn't have been ready to be mother to his five children or to be his loving wife, really, if I hadn't kept growing through scripture study."

Then Danny spoke: "There came a time in my life when things just didn't seem peaceful within me. A certain restlessness, with no apparent reason, made me feel a need to study the scriptures diligently. I even attended the stake class on the standard works, which was taught by an institute teacher. I kept the scriptures with me and read during my lunch hour or while I waited for appointments, and I listened to tapes here in my van while battling freeway traffic. For some reason, unknown to me then, I was intent upon learning all I could. And I came to love the scriptures. Then about ten months after I started my study, my wife was killed in an auto accident. I was devastated."

He wept sharing this part of his story, then continued. "The problems of my personal loss and of a motherless family were lifted by my knowledge of God's love for us and his wisdom. It is wonderful how I have been guided to all kinds of proper attitudes and decisions through scripture study—including marrying Anna."

In stormy seasons it helps immensely to read the scriptures reverently and prayerfully, pondering them for understanding. It helps in times of calmness to read with thanksgiving for blessings and peace. As you read, the plain and precious truths become known to you, mysteries unfold, wisdom floods your being.

Scripture study gives you instruction in righteousness, direction of duty, understanding of God's purposes and principles, examples of people and problem solving, comfort and strength. Study the scriptures so that you are prepared to meet adversity. The following scriptures may help you understand how important the scriptures can be: Isaiah 40:8; 2 Nephi 4:15; Mosiah 4:9; 3 Nephi 10:14; D&C 33:16; 130:18–21.

When you have made prayer and scripture study a part of your life, particularly in problem solving, the next step is to tidy up your life—repent, behave, become more conscientious about living exactly the word of God.

Study the scriptures to get answers and to get assurance. Don't forget the promises of God, because they give hope. Diligently searching the word of God and pondering what it means to you personally and listening with your inner soul can be an incredible benefit. I have had such joy from scripture study. Often it is as if the Lord himself is saying the words into my mind—such is the strength of the word of God, in print, to us.

Bridle All Your Passions

Shortly before my mother died, she began to wear down because of the struggle. She was nearly ninety. She had been ill for several years. She was in a convalescent institution, and much of the time she was miserable. But she refused to make other people miserable, too. So she bridled her passions as we are counseled to do in Alma 38:12. One of the last things I heard Mother say was, "I don't like it here much. I don't like what's happening to me. But I will behave, Elaine. I will behave!"

And she did.

That burden of dying became a blessing of beauty because of her attitude and her self-control. Mother had faith in God, all right. Prayer was her daily source of strength. She was a lifelong student of the scriptures. Still there are some things a person has to do largely alone. Being ready and dying right fall into that category. Mother wanted to die in the right way. "Do what is right; let the consequence follow" was her motto ("Do What Is Right," *Hymns,* 1985, no. 237).

Mother wasn't a fist-clencher or a molar-grinder about life. Mother was a smiler. When things came to a crisis, Mother would lift her chin, brightening her eye, and smile. She'd consciously pause a moment in the thick of trial, and she'd smile—and behave.

You might say that Mother had learned to bridle her passions, to try to keep the problem-causing attitudes mostly under control.

If you grieve overlong, if you lust, hate, envy, anger, criticize, pity self, or do anything similar to un-Christlike behavior, the Spirit of the Lord, which is love, is shut out. Bridling such attitudes makes it possible for you to *receive* the loving, healing gifts of God.

I have come to feel that this scripture, this godly counsel is powerful direction for polishing up our lives. And here is another one with a promise that helps us want to solve problems appropriately lest we shortchange future opportunities: "Sanctify yourselves: for to morrow the Lord will do wonders among you" (Joshua 3:5).

Bridle your passions, sanctify yourself, and you will be ready for the Lord to do wonders in your life and in your heart.

Repent

Sin is a burden.

We know that the plan of life calls for choices between the way of Christ and the way of Satan. Sin is forbidden because it is harmful. The wrong choice, then, is a burden of our own making.

If we want to turn the burden of sin into a blessing, we need to repent.

A young father and I sat in a fashionable restaurant in a fashionable city among animated people in fashionable clothing, celebrating the lunch hour. In the midst of the world we were apart from it. Our purpose in meeting and the tone of our talk had the deepest spiritual connotation.

He had sinned, had taken the route of confession, agony, excommunication, and finally, restoration of blessings. He had picked up the pieces of his life, church work, and family relationships. He'd married and had children.

Subsequent study and devotion to gospel life had brought about a mighty change in him. Now, matching himself against the Saints among us and the Savior as the ideal, he was suffering new feelings. Awareness of the risks he had taken with ugly sinning (that at one time had seemed so needful to him) frightened him. He was shocked now, that he had ever let it happen. Though he had been forgiven and welcomed back, he could not forgive himself. He was aghast at his actions and deeply sad. "I feel like Alma the younger," he explained. "Now that I have found myself again I panic to think what might have happened. I know how important it is to guard against any kind of estrangement from the Lord. This is my burden."

He went on to explain that he had been somewhat inactive and had participated in very questionable activities before he prepared for his mission. He served a fine mission and lived up to Church standards for a year or so after his return. "Gradually," he continued, "I was caught up in the enticements of the world—in all of this!" He gestured about us.

"It's difficult, isn't it?" I said. "Reentry into the real world from a spiritual life is a cultural shock, so to speak."

It was Emerson all over again—that it is easy to live in the world after the world's opinion, and it is easy to live on your own after your own. The challenge, oh, the painful challenge, is to live in the world and keep the pureness of your own values.

In today's world only a very committed person makes it.

This young father wanted to come to grips with a deep problem that he needed to keep under control. He did not live in a vacuum, and in his best moments he did not want to place his exaltation in jeopardy.

Misery is not happiness.

Succumbing to temptation is not peace.

Wickedness, the scriptures affirm, never was happiness.

The young father was anxious to talk for two reasons: he wanted to guard against further temptation in the area of deviate behavior, which was his weakness, and he wanted to be done with even the thought of it! He wanted to fortify himself spiritually and to watch and pray always.

And he wanted to help others from falling into the traps he had been caught in.

I speak of this incident in a section on repentance because repentance is the core of righting our life in order to bring peace. Trouble is sometimes of our own making. It may be a sin of impurity, or disobedience of some kind, or lack of love, or contention.

True repentance and peace come when we refuse to allow the things that matter most to be threatened by the things that matter least.

The young father I talked with can be very helpful to others who might be the target of Satan's team, which seems to be working overtime these days.

It is better never to have brought adversity upon ourselves at all by sin in any form. But if we learn from our mistakes and fortify ourselves against further sin, blessings can be found in service to others. As we succeed in avoiding the very appearance or thought of evil doing, we will be conscious of increased support from the Lord.

I shared an interesting quote from President Brigham Young with the young father fighting his way into confidence before the Lord and strength in the marketplace.

Said Brigham Young, "Keep your follies that do not concern others to yourselves, and keep your private wickedness as still as possible; hide it from the eyes of the public gaze as far as you can." "If you have sinned against one individual, take that person by yourselves and make your confession to him. And if you have sinned against your God, or against yourselves, confess to God, and keep the matter to yourselves, for I do not want to know anything about it." (In *Journal of Discourses,* 8:362, 361.)

I also shared with this father words from this lovely hymn:

> The wintry day, descending to its close,
> Invites all wearied nature to repose,
> And shades of night are falling dense and fast,
> Like sable curtains closing o'er the past
> Pale through the gloom the newly fallen snow
> Wraps in a shroud the silent earth below
> As tho 'twere mercy's hand had spread the pall,
> A symbol of forgiveness unto all.
> —Orson F. Whitney

Helping others when you've experienced adversity may include not talking about your personal problems in detail!

This counsel should not interfere with the established processes declared by prophets. When we have sinned—when we've done something that brings a particular kind of burden to loved ones, to our fellowmen, or to the Church, we must meet the requirements of that process so that our repentance may be complete.

When we have sinned, weeping may endure for a period of time, but joy comes with God's forgiveness in the beautiful morning after repentance. We should accept that gift and get on with life.

There isn't anyone who won't be tested. Even people whose lives seemed charmed have their day. Perhaps those who seem especially blessed are those who have learned to turn their burdens into blessings, who have learned to praise the Lord even in times of difficulty.

Scriptures regarding turning the burden of sin into a blessing through repentance should include all of 4 Nephi. The importance of repentance is stressed at least seventy-one times in the Doctrine and Covenants. Search for your favorites.

Forgiveness

When it comes to bridling our passions, repenting from sin, and turning burdens we're carrying into blessings for ourselves and others, forgiveness has to top any list of resolutions.

I visited with a man at his place of business on the day the newspapers had spread ugly reminders of the anniversary of his son's murder.

"How are you doing?" I asked him. "How do you cope—how can you stand this kind of heartbreak and frustration?"

"There is only one way to survive this kind of adversity," he replied. Then he leaned to whisper his answer in that public place. "Forgive," he said. "Forgive! And the blessings from heaven flood your life." It was the secret of his strength, his way of turning a burden into a blessing.

This man is an example of the believer in Christ.

What about irritating assaults on our peace; can we turn these burdens into blessings? Can we forgive the rebellious child? Can we forgive the persistent mother-in-law, the aggressive Church leader with whom we must serve? Can we be patient and understanding—forgiving—with the boss who is insensitive, the husband who doesn't understand a woman's work load, the wife who overspends?

The following scriptures can help us see how forgiveness can turn burdens into blessings: Ezekiel 18:22; Matthew 18:21; 1 Corinthians 10:11; 1 Timothy 4:12; Alma 36:12–20; D&C 58:42; 64:10; 98:40.

Seek Truth

Filtering truth out of the piles of information being circulated in our world is a major task. It is the object, in part, of problem solving. Whether your problem has to do with finances or relationships, sickness or sin, truth of the matter should be your goal. Seek not only what is right and what is wise, but what is truth. Eternal. God-given.

Wouldn't it be well for us, when adversity strikes, to remember the following:

1. We may not be able to change our circumstance, only our responses. We should seek applicable truth.

2. We can learn if we do not accept every truth to be of equal value. (Knowing that an egg gets hard when it boils so many minutes is not of the same value as knowing that smoking can cause cancer of the lung.)

3. All decisions and choices of any consequence should be made in the perspective of the gospel and with tender closeness to the Lord.

4. There is a difference between preference and principle, between opinion and a prophet's counsel, and between hearsay and truth.

Some scriptures to study regarding truth and problem solving include John 8:32; 1 John 1:8; 2 Nephi 9:40; D&C 93:24.

Take Charge of Your Life

When trouble comes, take charge of your life.

You can sulk and weep. You can run to the beleaguered bishop. You can talk over your problem with a neighbor or with others in the halls at church. You can make an appointment with a professional counselor. Or you can pray, study the scriptures, get your life in order, and then move forward to solve your problem with confidence before God.

Here's a story shared with me by a friend, Bill Ziegler. "An old cowboy said he had learned life's most important lessons from Hereford cows. All his life he had worked cattle ranches where winter storms took a heavy toll among the herds. Freezing rains whipped across the prairies. Howling, bitter winds piled snow into enormous drifts. Temperatures might drop quickly to below zero degrees. Flying ice cut into the flesh. In this maelstrom of nature's violence most cattle would turn their backs to the ice blasts and slowly drift downwind, mile upon mile. Finally, intercepted by a boundary fence, they would pile up against the barrier and die by the scores.

"But the Herefords acted differently. Cattle of this breed would instinctively head into the windward end of the range. There they would stand shoulder-to-shoulder facing the storm's blast, heads down against its onslaught.

" 'You always found the Herefords alive and well,' said the cowboy. 'I guess it's the greatest lesson I ever learned on the prairies—just face life's storms.' "

Now that is what is meant by taking charge of your life. Face up to it. Gird up your loins, pick up your wagon handle, and head west!

Or, like Edison, enjoy the drama and then get on with rebuilding your life.

I recall being impressed when President Spencer W. Kimball reminded women, "Each of you sisters has the right and the responsibility to direct your own life. But be not deceived; you must also be responsible for your choices. This is an eternal principle. The law of the harvest is ever in evidence." ("Privileges and Responsibilities of Sisters," *Ensign*, Nov. 1978, p. 105.)

So it is with problems and solutions.

You reap what you sow. You can also do what you want to about what happens to you—either adversity brought on by your own actions or the kind of trouble that comes unbidden, unannounced, or as a direct challenge from God.

Turning a burden of any kind into a blessing means shifting into high gear. We take charge of our life, which requires action of mind and body. Here are ten suggestions to help:

1. Be master of your fate. Be captain of your soul. This is your life. Get on with it until, at last, this, too, passes. Remember, endings—even death—make room for new beginnings.

2. Get a fresh perspective about yourself. Study your patriarchal blessing. Find out what Heavenly Father has to say to you—the promises and possibilities for your mission here on earth. Set some new goals or underscore some old ones. It will get your mind off old problems and turn hopelessness into hopefulness.

3. Get a new perspective about the particular adversity you are burdened with at the moment. Label the nature of it: can it be resolved or simply endured and accommodated? Was it self-induced or imposed by others? Was it God-given or circumstance?

4. Gather a written list of alternative solutions. Think big. Think wild. Think a lot! Then think prayerfully.

5. Make a choice.

6. Present your choice to the Lord. Spell it out. This is good therapy. The Lord will understand and keep your secrets. When you are ready, he'll help.

7. Listen to what you feel as you pray. Wait in patience for the Spirit to bring you answer.

8. Act with courage. No matter what, when you feel heavenly help, go forth with courage to tackle the problem.

9. Hang on, if that's all you can do for a time. But don't sink—swim, float, or at least kick a little, and look toward shore. It is there.

10. Pray in gratitude each step of the way.

The following scriptures will help you take charge and endure trials well: Matthew 10:11; 3 Nephi 15:9; D&C 121:8; 14:7–8; Articles of Faith 1:13.

Count Your Many Blessings

"And he who receiveth all things with thankfulness shall be made glorious; and the things of this earth shall be added unto him, even an hundred fold, yea, more" (D&C 78:19).

There is so much to be grateful for—even blessings from burdens are proof of that. We all know that happiness isn't the absence of adversity and suffering; it is the presence of God.

When such nice things come from such difficult struggles, we are almost coaxed to welcome adversity.

I listened intently to the story of an unhappy woman whose husband died and who had to work to support the family. All the time Shirley was praying for help, she heard the counsel to her spirit, "Go back to school." What she was praying for was more money to run her single-parent household!

Finally, though, she obeyed the prompting. She went back
to school. That was the beginning of a distinguished career
with children who needed special education. Oh, the good she
did and the awards she's won for innovative programs and
selfless hours in behalf of the handicapped.

A choice blessing came from her burden of death of a
spouse. Shirley is the first to admit God's hand in her life.
Things didn't turn out at all as she had planned as a dreamy-
eyed girl. But life has been wonderful and rewarding. She has
learned things that will stay with her eternally.

My much beloved mother-in-law died when the sixth of
our children was about to be born. He was a big baby. One
look at my large stomach proved that. And my large stomach
created a problem—I didn't have a suitable wrap to wear to
Nana Cannon's funeral. It was bitter cold weather. I could have
swathed myself in a blanket, but prominent people would be
participating and attending the funeral of a woman who had
been the wife of an Apostle. I wanted to go, but I knew that I
couldn't unless I had suitable clothing. I had a lot to be thankful for, but I wanted another blessing—I wanted to go to that
funeral of the woman I loved wearing suitable clothing for my
state of pregnancy!

I had heard a story once about an early general president of
the Young Women of the Church. It seems that when she
had a problem, she would tell her children not to disturb her as
she went into her bedroom to "talk some things over with
Heavenly Father." This story about Martha H. Tingey surfaced
in my mind during the sad time before the funeral.

The day before the services, I told our children that I was
going to talk with Heavenly Father about my needing an
appropriate wrap to wear to the funeral for Nana. They were to
be very good and not disturb me.

In my prayer, I explained my need. We were financially
strapped. I loved Nana. I didn't want to embarrass the family
by going with a blanket wrapped around me. I said that if
someone could be of help in solving my little problem then I'd
be mighty grateful. If that couldn't come about then would
Heavenly Father please bless me with my struggle of pride and
my disappointment!

When I came out of the bedroom, the four little children under six were crowded there. I had been somewhat conscious of their whisperings and jostlings while I was praying, I must confess. I noted that as I came out Christine went immediately into the bedroom and looked around. She was sure she'd see Heavenly Father. When she didn't, she asked me what he looked like!

The day of the funeral, when the early morning mail was delivered, there was a check among the letters from a magazine publishing company in New York. I had sent a manuscript to them many months before and had forgotten all about it—until the check came. It was for the exact amount of a coat I had been looking at the day before and simply did not have the money to buy. I hurried down to ZCMI and bought that coat just in time to go to the funeral.

This was an answer to prayer and I knew it! My heart was full of the knowledge that God lives and answers my prayers. He was mindful of a poor young mother filled with pride of appearance. That evening the children knelt with us in a prayer of thanksgiving for Nana and also for a witness of a loving Heavenly Father.

If I'd had a coat or money in the bank, our whole family would have been denied that blessing of faith when a mother's simple prayer was answered so promptly.

For those of us who are dependent upon a God we know and love, one to whom we turn when adversity strikes, it becomes increasingly clear that he lives and cares. The miracle stories, the sweet low-key responses to prayer, and the wondrous ways in which God deals with his troublesome children are proof of his goodness.

The way to turn burdens into blessings is to do all the things we have talked about in this book—when it is appropriate to do them. But always and forever, count your blessings. This is a great way to chase the sorrow, beat the blues, and lift the burden. There is hardship and anguish but look at all else that is going for us!

As you turn your burdens into blessings by counting your many blessings, include among them the following:

1. God lives and cares—even about small details.

2. We are his children and he loves us—not because we are so great but because he is.

3. God has a plan for his children which may be titled: *Even As I Am.*

4. His children come to understand the plan and purpose of life through problems.

5. Confirmation of the truth of the plan comes through the Holy Ghost.

6. Revelation of his will can come to us personally for our own well-being.

7. There are principles and promises and laws irrevocably decreed to help us become as he is.

Finally, as we consider the adversity in our lives, we may find strength in the following scriptures. "He giveth power to the faint; and to them that have no might he increaseth strength. . . . They that wait upon the Lord shall renew their strength; they shall mount up with wings as eagles; they shall run, and not be weary; and they shall walk, and not faint." (Isaiah 40:29, 31.)

"But we glory in tribulations also: knowing that tribulations worketh patience; and patience, experience; and experience, hope: and hope maketh not ashamed; because the love of God is shed abroad" (Romans 5:3–5).

Over the years I repeatedly have been comforted and directed by such scriptures as the above. But there is one section of the Book of Mormon that absolutely has been my joy to refer to in time of need and to share with others who are hurting, weeping, distraught, bewildered, and weary of the battle. It is found in Mosiah 24 when the children of God cried out because their afflictions were great and Amulon put guards over the people to watch them so that anyone found calling upon God to help them would be put to death. The account tells us that the people didn't raise their voices to the Lord their God. Instead they poured out their hearts to God, and he knew the thoughts of their hearts.

And the voice of the Lord came to them in their terrible times, and they heard his voice, telling them to be of good comfort and to lift up their heads for he was mindful of them.

Then these following words from God are those particularly precious to anyone who feels forgotten in affliction or bereft of ever overcoming such burdens. I strongly suggest that you read these lines carefully for your own benefit, for I am certain that such a promise applies to us as much in our day, in our adversity, as to those of another generation.

"And I will also ease the burdens which are put upon your shoulders, that even you cannot feel them upon your backs, even while you are in bondage; and this will I do that ye may stand as witnesses for me hereafter, and that ye may know of a surety that I, the Lord God, do visit my people in their afflictions. And . . . the Lord did strengthen them that they could bear up their burdens with ease, and they did submit cheerfully and with patience to all the will of the Lord." (Mosiah 24:14–15.)

The *chambered nautilus* suggests that we can leave our outgrown shell by life's unresting sea of experiences; we can move to another life freed by lessons learned, polished by adversity well handled.

Adversity? Who needs it? Everyone, because adversity well handled is really blessings in disguise. Perhaps this book should be retitled *In Gratitude to God!*

For after much tribulation
come the blessings.

—D&C 58:4

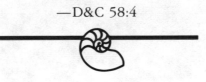

Index

Responsibility, 5–6, 34
Revelation, personal, 138
Rime of the Ancient Mariner, The
  (poem), 99
Russian peasants, 83

— S —

Sacrament, 35–36
Sacrifice, 5, 82, 91
Satan, 7, 34, 35, 46, 107, 130
  buffetings of, 13
Schulz, Charles, 104
Scripture study, 12, 35, 62, 69, 91,
  109, 124, 126–28, 133
Self-control, 124, 128–29
Self-esteem, 4, 70–71
Selfishness, 11
Self-pity, 5, 68, 104–5, 107, 128
Self-worth, 5
Senility, 93
Service, 5, 6, 69, 79, 130
  capacity for, increased through
  adversity, 39–47
Shakespeare, William, *Hamlet,*
  52–53
  King Henry the Fifth, 121
  Much Ado About Nothing, 84
Sin, 11–16, 90–91, 129–32
Singing, 124–25
Single parents, 4, 70, 74, 135–36
Single women, 5, 67–70, 96–97,
  108–9, 117–18, 126–27
Slaves, 83
Smith, Emma, 57, 83
Smith, Joseph, 57, 83
  on tribulation, 30
  suffering of, 43, 44
Smith, Joseph F., on purpose of
  life, 24
Snow, Eliza R., "Though Deepen-
  ing Trials," 118
Soldiers, 40
Songs, 124–25
Starvation, 98
Stevenson, Robert Louis, 3–4
Suffering, 42–44, 98
Suicide, 44–45, 56, 73–74
Surgery, 60–61

— T —

Tabernacle, 93–94
Taylor, John, 62
Teenagers, 125
Temple dedications, 96
Temple marriage, 55, 90–91, 110
Temple ordinances, 69
Temptation, 16, 34, 44, 83, 91,
  93, 119, 130
Ten Commandments, 12
Testimony, 6, 41, 44, 61, 89, 90,
  94
Teton Dam disaster, 29–30
Thayne, Emma Lou, hymn, 118
"The Lord Is My Shepherd"
  (hymn), 117
"The Wintry Day, Descending to
  Its Close" (hymn), 131
"Though Deepening Trials"
  (hymn), 118
Tingey, Martha H., 136
Torture, 45, 99
Tribulation, 52
Trustworthiness, 22, 29–36, 41,
  74, 83, 120
Truth, seeking, 16, 124, 132–33
Tuttle, A. Theodore, 90

— U —

Understanding, 4, 5, 22
  increased through adversity,
  39–47
Unemployment, 31–32
Unwed mothers, 90–93

— V —

Vicar of Wakefield, The (book), 6
Vision, 113–14
Visiting teachers, 72

— W —

Walker, Esther Mary, poem, 106
Wars, 120
Wealth, 14, 54
Welfare, church, 78–79